Oxfordshii
of the
Supernatural

Betty Puttick

COUNTRYSIDE BOOKS
NEWBURY, BERKSHIRE

First published 2003
© Betty Puttick 2003

COUNTRYSIDE BOOKS
3 Catherine Road
Newbury, Berkshire

To view our complete range of books,
please visit us at
www.countrysidebooks.co.uk

ISBN 1 85306 811 X

Designed by Graham Whiteman
Cover design by Peter Davies, Nautilus Design

Produced through MRM Associates Ltd., Reading
Typeset by Mac Style Ltd, Scarborough, N. Yorkshire
Printed by J.W. Arrowsmith Ltd., Bristol

Contents

Introduction

Most people are interested in ghosts, even if they don't believe in them, and curiosity about the paranormal is very strong these days. Whereas people who have experienced a brush with the supernatural once kept quiet about it lest they should seem a little strange, today when the conversation turns to ghosts and hauntings, it often seems that everyone has a tale to tell.

But what are ghosts? Some seem no more than a kind of faded old photograph, as if over time all the colour has drained out of them. Perhaps that is why there are so many grey ladies and misty monks. Others repeatedly re-enact a dramatic happening of long ago, and it seems to any bemused witness as if they had tuned into what someone called 'the cinema of time'. Then there are the earthbound spirits, lost unhappy souls tied by some powerful emotions such as hate, anger or passionate love to a world they should have left behind. Other ghosts are paying just a fleeting visit to those they love – either at the time of death, or later.

The sheer variety of every aspect of the paranormal illustrates how little we know about the eternal mystery of what happens to us after death. There will always be sceptics who dismiss the whole subject as superstitious nonsense, but by doing this they are ignoring the vast bulk of evidence.

Oxfordshire has a wide range of hauntings and apparitions – from a 12th century king's mistress, who frequently pops into her local, to a Second World War bomber pilot. Many of the picturesque old Cotswold pubs have ghosts, and the roads are busy with phantom vehicles both ancient and modern. A visit to Wychwood Forest might be nothing but a pleasant woodland stroll, or you could meet the Devil's coach on the lookout for souls, or Amy Robsart with her dire warning of death. There are shadowy monks everywhere, a rather damp phantom hitch-hiker, ancient mysteries and even a romance with a ghost. And more ... read on.

Happy ghost hunting!

Betty Puttick

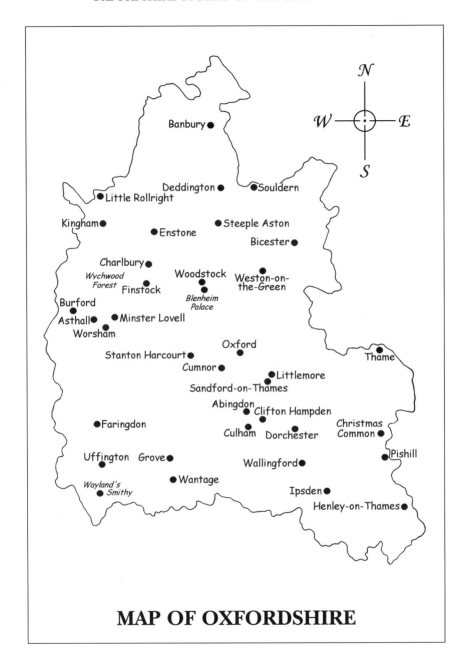

MAP OF OXFORDSHIRE

1

The House in Magpie Lane

Magpie Lane is a turning off Oxford's High Street, and there you will find an old three-storey Elizabethan house that was once Barclays Bank and is now the Old Bank Hotel. The house has a well-known ghost with a sad story dating back to the Civil War, when Charles I and his wife, Henrietta Maria, had their court for a time in Oxford. Prudence Burcote was a Puritan, and a supporter of Cromwell, and was living at that time in the house in Magpie Lane. Under what circumstances she came to fall in love with a Royalist charmer, said to be a member of the Queen's household, is not known but it was obviously a love story destined to have an unhappy ending.

How one would like to know more about this intriguing love affair, but all we are told is that Prudence died of a broken heart.

Some years ago when the house was a private residence, a Cornish couple moved in. They had heard that Prudence was already in residence, and were not worried about such a gentle spirit sharing their home. It was quite soon after their arrival that Mrs B first encountered Prudence. She was ironing in the kitchen when she looked up and saw someone watching her. As the figure was standing between the ironing board and the window, Mrs B realised this was no casual caller who had walked through the door from the street.

Mrs B knew at once that she was looking at Prudence Burcote, although as she said at the time, the ghost was not as she had imagined her. 'She was of medium height, very sallow, wearing a long brown dress with a white fichu. It was the fichu

7

that particularly surprised me, as I had imagined her with a large white Puritan collar. Her expression was sad. We stood there looking at each other for some minutes, or so it seemed. Then she disappeared.'

Oddly enough, Prudence never made another appearance, so Mr B never encountered their ghost, although he had no doubt that his wife had seen her. But Prudence made herself felt in other ways, particularly one that seems to be a favourite with many supernatural visitors. She loved to play with the electricity, and Mr and Mrs B frequently found the lights switched on in the morning although they knew that they had been switched off when they went to bed. Sometimes just as they were settling down they would suddenly notice a chink of light under the bedroom door as the landing light went on. And once when they were on holiday a neighbour noticed the house ablaze with light. Luckily there were no intruders, it was just Prudence amusing herself!

Despite the increased electricity bills, Mr and Mrs B were happy with their supernatural lodger, and said that her presence gave the house a warm, lived-in feeling whenever they returned after an absence.

Soon after they moved into the house in Magpie Lane, they gave a sherry party and after the guests had gone Mr B went round collecting the glasses. He found he had one short despite a thorough search, so he washed the glasses he had, and on returning to the drawing room to his surprise there in full view was the missing glass. The next time they had guests the same thing happened. One glass was missing, but when he returned to the drawing room there it was in the middle of the room on a small table. There was no way he could have overlooked it before, so they came to the conclusion that perhaps Puritan Prudence was hinting that she did not approve of sherry parties.

When the building became a bank the staff were aware of a presence at times, mostly footsteps when no one was there, or the whisper of ghostly skirts. In a busy hotel, as the house is now, perhaps sounds like these go unnoticed – or has anyone come across a lady in brown with a white fichu and a sad expression and a penchant for hiding wine glasses?

2

❖❖❖❖❖❖❖❖❖❖❖❖❖❖❖

On the Road

Most motorists would agree that today's highways have enough hazards without worrying about the possibility of meeting a spectral stagecoach drawn by headless horses, or a phantom hitch-hiker! And yet strange encounters do happen without warning in country lanes and motorways alike, with ghostly jaywalkers who unexpectedly dash out in front of the car; disappearing hitch-hikers; mysterious vehicles of another period, apparently bent on a head-on collision; shadowy horses and riders; hooded monks and white ladies all leaving worried motorists wondering if they were dreaming. And yet they know that something unusual happened – but what?

It was a foggy night in November 1983 when a lady called Mrs Brason drove along the Bicester to Banbury road near Souldern. She noticed a car ahead of her, and as she drew nearer it appeared to be an old type of estate car, black with wooden strips. It had no lights, which made her nervous of overtaking in the fog, but another car was approaching fast behind her and she decided that when it overtook the estate car, she would follow it. But as she drew out she was stunned to find that there was now no estate car, it had completely vanished, although there was no side road where it could have turned off.

Mrs Brason had never forgotten this strange incident, and after she told her story on Radio Oxford in January 1996 she was interested to find that her experience had not been unique. A listener called Ken Fowler telephoned her after the broadcast to describe his own encounter on the same road near the Bear pub at Souldern.

It happened in 1963, on another foggy November night, when Mr Fowler was 17. He was riding his motorcycle when he, too, saw the mysterious vehicle – which he recognised as a Morris 1000 Traveller – but in his case the car with no headlights was in the middle of the road facing him. Instinctively he slowed down as he approached it, and when he got within about 20 yards, it disappeared right before his eyes.

When I visited the Souldern area in the autumn of 2002 while researching this book, I intended to go to the Bear pub, hoping I might learn that other travellers on the Bicester to Banbury road had encountered the phantom Morris 1000 Traveller and perhaps gone into the Bear for a drink and told their story. But it was not to be – I found that as a pub the Bear was no more; it was now a private house.

But surely these two encounters so far apart were not the only times the mystery Morris made an appearance? If one foggy night the same thing has happened to you, it would be interesting to know!

In Anne Mitchell's book *Ghosts Along the Thames*, she describes what happened to a couple many years ago as they drove towards a railway bridge at Littlemore, near Oxford. Suddenly a girl on a bicycle appeared, riding straight towards the car. The wife screamed 'Mind that girl' as her husband did not appear to have noticed the cyclist, and he instinctively jammed on the brake when he saw the girl, who was almost on the bonnet of the car. As he braked she disappeared from sight, and when the car stopped the couple got out, terrified at what they expected to find.

But there was nothing! They looked beneath the car, sure that the girl cyclist could not have escaped injury, but there was no sign of either bicycle or rider, or any evidence of damage to their vehicle.

The phantom hitch-hiker has become as much a classic in the literature of hauntings as monks, nuns and white ladies, and there are stories from all over the world in which a driver picks up a hitch-hiker from the roadside, who then mysteriously disappears during the course of the journey. Some accounts are linked to a fatal accident which once happened at the site, and are associated with the victim, but there appears to be no such incident to explain the young girl's apparition that has sometimes been seen by the roadside near Asthall Manor. Her clothes and appearance suggest that she is a gypsy and in recent times, in the mid-1990s, drivers who have given her a lift all have a similar tale to tell.

It was an evening in October when a driver noticed a figure by the side of the road. She had dark shoulder length hair, olive skin and a gypsy-like appearance, and she had moved into the middle of the road, waving to him to stop. He drew up and asked her what was the matter. She made no reply but walked round to the passenger door, which he opened, and got into the car. It had been raining, but the girl was more than just damp, she was completely soaking wet, her hair dripping down over her face as if she had been in the river. The driver said she must get home as soon as possible or she would catch pneumonia but she made no reply, simply pointing ahead. He was conscious of an overwhelming feeling of anxiety at the strangeness of the situation, when suddenly the girl spoke for the first time. 'It's too late, he's gone,' she said, and at that she disappeared.

The driver arrived home feeling shaken by his unlikely experience, but it was some time before he could tell anyone about it.

It was also wet on an afternoon in March when a woman set off from Burford to pick up her son from school. She had just passed Asthall Manor when she noticed a young gypsy girl in the road waving to her to stop. As she drew up she could see that the gypsy was soaking wet, and before she could speak the girl said, 'You got my message then?' She walked round to the passenger side of the car, and when the driver opened the door she got in. It was obvious that she was distressed and when the driver asked, 'What message? Where do you want to go?' the gypsy simply stared silently back at her with an agonised expression. Then suddenly she said, 'The water, the river – he's gone,' and without another word she disappeared, leaving just a wet car seat and a pool of water on the floor where she had been.

The driver continued on her journey, bemused by this experience, and like the driver mentioned above, felt unable to tell anyone what had happened for some time.

What is the story behind the appearances of the gypsy hitch-hiker on that particular stretch of road near Asthall Manor? Her soaking wet appearance suggests a connection with the river Windrush nearby. Her brief remark to both drivers gives the impression that someone had drowned in the river – perhaps her efforts to save them were fruitless, and sorrow has kept her forever earthbound to the site of the tragedy? Perhaps we may never know.

Burford has its own terror, all the more alarming because it is so nebulous.

It is like a black cloud and motorists who drive through it experience a feeling of inexplicable alarm, and it is said that animals who find themselves surrounded by it become frantic with fear. I'm sorry I can't tell you exactly where you may encounter this frightening miasma, but I feel sure you will know when you do …

The Rollright Stones near Little Rollright (see chapter 12) are, of course, long associated with ancient and mysterious stories, and in his book *Places of Power* Paul Devereux tells that in 1980, on the 100 yard stretch of road beside the Stones, there were three reports of apparently paranormal happenings in the space of a fortnight. One man saw a huge dog pass by his van and promptly vanish. Another man saw a car with two people inside pass by, and also disappear. And for someone else it was the unexpected sight of a traditional style gypsy caravan – there one moment and gone the next!

According to Paul Devereux, that particular stretch of road exhibited a high degree of natural radioactivity, presumably due to particularly active granite in its foundation.

Coaches and horses not of this world have for centuries surprised travellers and one in particular is said to frequent mysterious Wychwood Forest. This is a smart black four-wheeler with a scarlet crest; it is drawn by two horses and driven by Lucifer himself. His Satanic Majesty comes on the hunt for souls every seven years, but who knows which is the seventh year? Perhaps it is best to proceed very carefully when you're in the area.

A phantom coach also haunts the road between Finstock and Charlbury (see Chapter 12), but often there is nothing to be seen, just the sound of horses' hooves and the rumble of an invisible vehicle.

There is a story of a mother and her little boy who were walking towards the bridge near Finstock when they heard the sounds of a coach and horses approaching, but nothing arrived so they crossed the bridge. Then, although the mother could see nothing, the child told her that the lady in the coach was signalling to him to come closer. This naturally frightened the mother, who held on tightly to her son. She heard the sound of horses stamping as if a coach had drawn up, and then the unmistakable sound of a coach setting off again.

Although she could still see nothing, she asked the boy what he had seen and he described a green coach with a lady sitting in it, with two men on the front. The lady was wearing a big hat with feathers, and a black jacket with a white blouse. He said the lady was crying and had beckoned him and held out her hands to him and was angry when his mother would not allow him to go to her.

Fleeting visions of various kinds occur on many roads, as frequent eye witness accounts testify, and sometimes there is a local story that seems to account for what is seen. Does the Littlemore cyclist only ride hellbent for disaster when a car appears? Or is she always there, even when there is no other traffic? It was a foggy night on both recorded occasions when the Morris Traveller was seen on the Bicester to Banbury road. Is it there at other times, or were these appearances marking the anniversary of an accident on a night like that sometime in the past?

There are reports of another phantom vehicle on the A4260 between Banbury and Oxford. It was in 1978 that a young woman reporter was travelling along this road one night when she had to brake suddenly on coming upon a red sports car stationary in the middle of the road. It had obviously been damaged in an accident, and Sue Ede had a lucky escape as she was forced to stop so suddenly that the driver behind almost collided with her.

Badly shaken she got out of her car, but when she turned round she could hardly believe her eyes as there was now no trace of the damaged sports car. It had vanished. Completely at a loss as to what had happened, Sue drove on, and to her amazement after two miles there was the same red sports car, once again in the middle of the road. And as before, she had scarcely seen it before it disappeared yet again.

She made attempts to find out more about the vanishing vehicle, and was told that an American serviceman was said to have been in a fatal accident in a sports car on that road some years before. One may ask why a particular accident out of so many that occur should sometimes be recalled with such alarming reality, but there is really no answer. These strange happenings join a long list of phantom vehicles and spectral figures encountered on England's highways and byways and remain an intriguing mystery.

3

The Crime of Mary Blandy

Mary Blandy, the notorious Henley on Thames poisoner, is a restless ghost. Since she was hanged in 1752 for putting an end to her father, she has returned to many of her former haunts. She has been seen on the execution mound behind Westgate shopping centre in Oxford where she met her death, and, although her home in Hart Street, Henley was later demolished and another house built on this site, sometimes Mary's ghost is said to stand beneath an old mulberry tree at the end of the garden.

But her most dramatic appearances were at Henley's Kenton Theatre in 1969. *The Hanging Wood*, a play by Joan Morgan based on Mary Blandy's story, was in rehearsal at the theatre when people began to notice various odd happenings. Doors would open by themselves, then slam shut suddenly, and lights came on and off without human intervention. Then the cast were aware of the figure of a woman standing at the back of the theatre, apparently watching the rehearsals, but whenever anyone approached her she faded away into the shadows and was gone. All this reminded Miss Morgan that some years previously, when a dramatised version of Mary Blandy's trial was performed at Henley Town Hall, a similar figure had been seen at the back of the hall while rehearsals were going on.

Was it the ghost of Mary Blandy? Naturally members of the cast thought it might be, and one evening as they sat drinking coffee and talking about her, something happened to shake the sceptics among them. Someone had put a cup down on the floor, and, as the cast watched in stunned amazement, it rose right up several inches above the floor and then dashed down again to break into pieces.

Apparently, in her lifetime Mary Blandy used to visit Turville Court in the Hambledon Valley, and her ghost on a white horse has sometimes been seen in Churchfield Wood there. Local people also say that she has often been seen walking down a lane that leads to Dolsden Farm, which would have been a bridlepath in her day. In Elizabeth Wiltshire's booklet *Valley Ghosts and Legends*, she tells of her grandfather's encounter with Mary Blandy's ghost one clear moonlight night.

The lane up from Dolsden Farm is steep and Mr Wiltshire was pushing his bicycle along it when he saw someone approaching. In the bright moonlight he could see that it was a woman in strangely old-fashioned clothes and as he got nearer he could hear the rustle of her skirts, It was late for a woman to be out alone, and thinking she might be afraid at meeting a man in that lonely lane he did not acknowledge her presence as they drew level. On second thoughts he realised it might have been more reassuring if he had raised his cap and said 'Goodnight', so he turned, and to his surprise, although he could still hear the rustle of her skirt, the figure had vanished. He hurried home, white and shaken, and told his wife, 'I've seen a ghost!'

In *The Buckinghamshire Dialect*, H. Harman recounts another Turville resident's experience: 'One dark night my wife and I were walking down the road … we felt something pass us and heard the rustling of a silk dress. My wife nearly fainted … I turned to see what it was but could see nothing. It really upset my wife and she has never forgotten it.'

Mary's father, Francis Blandy, was a solicitor and the Henley Town Clerk, a busy and prosperous man, ambitious that his only daughter, born in 1720, should make an advantageous marriage. With this in mind he did nothing to discount local rumours that Mary's future inheritance would be in the region of £10,000. So Mary was considered quite a 'catch', although she was no beauty. In fact, although she had a good figure and striking black eyes, her face was described as 'rather ordinary, not improved by the results of smallpox'.

In the summer of 1746 Mary and her parents were invited to dinner at Paradise House, the home of General Mark Kerr. Another guest was Captain William Henry Cranstoun, in Henley on a recruiting mission, and he and Mary were mutually attracted. Cranstoun must have had a charm which did not rely on his physical appearance, as he is described as being short and ordinary looking, with sandy hair, small weak eyes, a freckled and pitted skin and 'clumsy legs'. He was known to have a roving eye, but to Mr and Mrs Blandy he was highly eligible due to the fact that he was the fifth son of a Scottish peer, Lord Cranstoun.

During the summer of 1747, when Cranstoun again visited Henley, he declared his love for Mary. Mary accepted his proposal, and her parents welcomed him with open arms, arranging for him to come to stay with them for a time. But nemesis in the shape of a letter from a relative of Cranstoun's soon followed. It informed Mr Blandy that Cranstoun already had a wife and child in Scotland. He had married Anne Murray in 1744, but as she was a Jacobite and a Roman Catholic, it had been kept secret lest it damaged his chances of promotion.

Mr Blandy was understandably furious, but Mary and her mother believed Cranstoun's protestations that the marriage would soon be annulled. However, his attempts to get his marriage contract put aside failed; the court declared him legally married and he was ordered to pay his wife an annuity, an unwelcome outcome that he kept to himself. Mrs Blandy's health was deteriorating, and in September 1749 she died. Cranstoun had lost an ally, and Mr Blandy now became increasingly unfriendly towards Cranstoun, making no secret of the fact that his visits to the house were unwelcome.

Cranstoun told Mary about a wise woman he knew in Scotland whose 'love powders' acted like magic, and promised that if she gave some to her father they would make him more amenable to their relationship. Mary had her doubts, until she recalled that one day when her father had been in a particularly angry mood

Cranstoun had put some of his magic powder into Mr Blandy's tea, and the old man had become much more cheerful. This convinced her that her plausible lover could be right after all.

Cranstoun returned to Scotland early in 1751, from where he sent Mary some of the 'love philtres' to give to her father, with the result that Mr Blandy became very ill with pain and sickness. Their maid, Susan, happened to taste a cup of tea intended for Mr Blandy and was ill for a week afterwards. And on another occasion the family's old charwoman drank some of his tea, with similar results.

On 5th August 1751 Mary gave her father some gruel for his supper and he became so ill in the night that they had to call the apothecary. Next day poor Mr Blandy was given more gruel, with the same results, and later when the cook brought the remains of his supper downstairs, the charwoman ate it and became violently sick.

When Mary wanted to give her father more of the same gruel the maid protested that it was now too stale. She and the cook were becoming suspicious, and when they examined the gruel pan they discovered some white, gritty substance at the bottom. They hid the pan in a locked cupboard overnight.

Mary's uncle, the Revd Stevens, arrived on 9th August, and Susan, the maid, told him about their suspicions. And the next day they told Mr Blandy that they thought he was being poisoned, but even so the old man trustingly drank the tea Mary gave him at breakfast, simply complaining that it had a gritty taste.

In the light of these events it is hard to believe that Mary did not know the true nature of Cranstoun's 'magic' powders. The fact that Susan and the cook were eyeing her with suspicion was not lost on her, and she took Cranstoun's letters and what was left of the powder and threw everything on the kitchen fire. But with great presence of mind the cook immediately put some more coal on the fire, and when Mary had gone was able to rescue the paper packet still containing some of the white powder.

Meanwhile, Mr Blandy was deteriorating fast, and the doctor had no doubt that his patient had been poisoned. When he left, he took with him the sediment from the gruel pan and the packet the cook had rescued from the fire.

Mr Blandy died on 14th August 1751, forgiving his daughter and warning her yet again about the treacherous Cranstoun. Too late, Mary Blandy realised what she had done, and full of remorse she ran from the house, down Hart Street and over the bridge to the Angel Inn. But angry Henley residents followed her there, and she was taken to Oxford, where she went on trial for murder on 29th February 1752.

She was found guilty, and on 6th April, protesting her innocence to the last, she was publicly hanged in front of Oxford Castle from a gallows consisting of a wooden beam placed between two trees. Mary died bravely, and, obviously still concerned with her modesty at such a traumatic moment, her last request was: 'For the sake of decency gentlemen, don't hang me high.' Her body was brought back to Henley and buried at night between the graves of her parents in the presence of an enormous crowd of local people. Was it just curiosity that brought them there, or did they see her not as a murderer, but rather as an innocent girl misled by a heartless villain?

Cranstoun himself did not live long after her. On 2nd December in the same year he died at Furnes, near Dunkirk, of a strange illness which caused him to swell enormously and expire in great agony. He was 46 years old.

Until a few years ago there was apparently no known portrait of Mary Blandy in her home town, but in 1987 the Hon. Georgina Stonor discovered a print of her, which she presented to the town the following year. One must admit that if this is a true likeness Mary has a cool and calculating expression, and her heavily lidded eyes appear to view the world with deep suspicion. Surely a woman like that would have suspected that Cranstoun's 'love philtres' were some kind of deadly poison? Whatever the truth of Mary's guilt or innocence, it seems from her many subsequent appearances in a variety of locations that her spirit is still in a restless state of agitation.

4

Priests, Monks and Naughty Nuns

Weston Manor in Weston-on-the-Green is a fine Tudor house, now an hotel, but in the 12th century it was a monastery with the not unusual story of clandestine goings-on between the monks and nuns. It has had quite a colourful past, especially in the Civil War, when Prince Rupert hid there after his defeat at the Battle of Islip. Apparently General Fairfax, Cromwell's commander, also arrived at the manor and the story goes that the room where he slept was the one in which the Prince was taking cover in the chimney. While Fairfax was still sleeping in the morning Prince Rupert disguised himself as a dairymaid and made his escape to Oxford.

Weston Manor Hotel is reputedly haunted by the nun they call Mad Maude, who fell in love with one of the monks and in her passion for him forgot her vow of chastity. She was caught in the monk's cell one night and paid a terrible price, being tried and burnt at the stake in the monastery's grounds. There is no information about the fate of the monk.

The haunted room is the best bedroom, known as the Oak Room, which has a handsome antique four poster bed and is thought to be the site of the cramped and chilly cell where Maude was discovered with her lover on that fateful night. Many people who have occupied the Oak Room have experienced a frightening sense of a hostile presence, a feeling that there is something supernatural at large. They cannot see it, but know that it is definitely malevolent.

It is reported that in September 1975 a British Tourist Authority representative stayed at Weston Manor to investigate the stories that the Oak Room was haunted and he did experience an unusual sensation of heat during the night. He said, 'I cannot remember even in Africa such a close and oppressive atmosphere. I was not only hot, but unable to breathe properly.' Came the dawn and the temperature dropped back to normal. Was Maude giving the bedroom's occupant a hint of the terrible choking heat she suffered as the flames engulfed her?

There are other ghost stories at the manor – some say the tower is haunted by the ghost of a dairymaid who fell from there to her death, possibly committing suicide. The other manifestation is a phantom coach and horses, which occasionally drives into the yard at the back, and disappears.

In Banbury, Whateley Hall Hotel is haunted by a priest who was literally frightened to death! It used to be known as the Three Tuns, and back in 1687 during times of religious persecution, Catholics used a room there for their clandestine meetings. They had their secret escape route of hidden tunnels through which they could reach the street if a signal told them that danger threatened. But one night a young servant at the inn rang the alarm bell for a joke, which proved to be too much for the priest, who suffered a terror attack and died. It is said that Father Bernard has haunted the staircase ever since.

Another priest came to a sad end at the Crown at Christmas Common, Pishill. This had an exceptionally large priest hole under the roof, which proved a vital hideaway for Catholics at the time of the Reformation.

Father Dominique emerged from his hiding place one day at the same time as a young woman called Elizabeth arrived to stay at the inn. Their eyes met and they fell in love, and during her stay their romantic trysts continued, despite the danger that Dominique could be discovered at any time, and regardless of his vow of chastity, which meant that their love had no future.

A young aristocrat called at the inn for a meal one day, and noticing the lovely Elizabeth, he made advances to her, but when she was unmistakably unimpressed by his compliments he became aggressive and insulting. Dominique in his hiding place could hear what was going on, and regardless of danger he caught up a sword from the wall, ran downstairs and challenged the young man to a duel. Sadly for the priest, the young man was a much more skilled swordsman and Dominique's gallantry and love for Elizabeth was not enough to save him. A ghost in a black cloak has haunted the inn ever since the fatal duel and there are sometimes unexplained noises from the area beneath the roof.

Langstone Priory at Kingham used to be known as the Langstone Arms Hotel and is now an old people's home. It is said that its foundations are much older than the present building, and its cellars are believed to have been connected by a secret passage to Bruern Abbey. It was in the 1960s that a ghost was particularly active, appearing every ten days or so. It announced its arrival by the sound of shuffling footsteps and a polite cough, and the figure of what appeared to be an old woman wearing some kind of headdress was seen, often in room no. 1 of the hotel. Dogs, who frequently seem to be aware of the supernatural, have shown signs of terror when the ghost was about and have refused to go into the haunted room. Because of the supposed connection with Bruern Abbey it has been suggested that the ghost is a nun.

The Bull Inn, Henley on Thames, has an unusual form of haunting. Sometimes in a certain area of the bar there is the inexplicable smell of burnt candles. A guest staying there also reported waking in the night to find a cowled figure bending over his bed.

In the realm of the supernatural, monks are as ubiquitous as white ladies and at Burford Priory the sound of singing near the old monks' graveyard has been heard, and the tolling of a bell at 2 am, the time when the monks would have been woken for their devotions. There are also reports of the sighting of a 'little brown monk'.

Another ghost at the priory is described as a gamekeeper, complete with blunderbuss or flintlock gun, who walks regardless through any obstruction in his path. There is a story that this man was hanged for a crime he did not commit. In 1697 Lord Abercromb had a serious argument with John Pryor, and shortly afterwards Pryor was found dead. Lord Abercromb was charged with the murder, but found not guilty, and the gamekeeper was hanged instead. His ghost was seen in the priory vegetable garden at first, and it is thought that the nuns must have prayed for his soul, as, although he continued to appear for a time, he has not been seen since 1949.

5

◆◆◆◆◆◆◆◆◆◆◆◆◆◆◆◆

A Royal Romance

Although it is hundreds of years since it happened, the story of Henry II, the beautiful woman known as Fair Rosamund and his jealous vengeful Queen, Eleanor of Aquitaine, has never been forgotten. Indeed even today in the Wolvercote area people have encountered a ghostly white lady who haunts the ancient ruins of Godstow Nunnery and the nearby Trout Inn, and everyone believes her to be the tragic heroine of one of history's most romantic liaisons.

From the time of the Norman kings the forest area around Woodstock was a royal hunting ground, and the original hunting lodge grew into a splendid residence over the years, a favourite venue for royalty until the Civil War, when it was captured by Cromwell. After the Battle of Blenheim, Queen Anne gave the old Woodstock Palace, by then virtually a ruin, to John Churchill, the Duke of Marlborough, and when the architect John Vanbrugh embarked on the building of Blenheim, Sarah, Duchess of Marlborough insisted that what remained of the former palace should be demolished. Today there is just a stone commemorating it, and a spring in the grounds of Blenheim Park that is known as Rosamund's Well.

Rosamund de Clifford was the dearly loved mistress of Henry II, who cherished her safety by installing her in a secret bower in the grounds of Woodstock Palace, protected by one of his knights, Sir Thomas, within a labyrinth of intricate pathways through which the way could only be found with the aid of a silver thread. Their relationships lasted for several years, during which time Rosamund bore the King two sons.

One can imagine that, despite her love for Henry, Rosamund must have led rather a lonely life in her secret hideaway, and, when in 1175 the king was about to leave for France to go to war against his son, Rosamund begged him to let her go too, but he would not consider this, little realising that he was leaving his beloved to the tender mercies of his jealous wife.

With Henry out of the country Eleanor lost no time in disposing of Sir Thomas, and once in possession of the vital thread, she was able to find her way through the maze to Rosamund; then she forced her rival to drink from a poisoned chalice, with fatal results.

Rosamund's coffin was taken by the nuns to nearby Godstow Nunnery, where Henry erected a splendid tomb in honour of his lost love. So was that the end of the beautiful lady always known as Fair Rosamund? At the time of the Dissolution of the Monasteries in the 16th century Rosamund's tomb was vandalised, after which her ghost appeared in the ruins of Godstow Nunnery and the river area. Locals and staff say that she regularly walks at the nearby Trout Inn, where she is seen from the knees upwards as she is on the original floor, which today has been raised by the addition of flagstones.

One evening in May 2000, after the pub was closed, a member of the staff reported: 'I was putting all the chairs up on the tables, and looked to my right to see if the chairs had been put up in the green [the area of the pub that is the oldest]. As I looked down the building and through the doorway I saw a figure move across on the other side of the entrance. I thought it was one of my colleagues but when I went down there, there was no one in the room. I went back to the main part of the pub where all the other staff were, and no one had been in that area for at least twenty minutes. Immediately after I saw this figure there was a very cold spot where I had seen her.'

Other staff and customers have noticed unexplained cold patches, and sometimes a sweet flowery smell. Also, rather unexpectedly for such a charming ghost, Rosamund is sometimes blamed for knocking wine bottles off tables, and giving people a fright by standing behind them. There have also been sightings of the apparition of a lovely fair haired young lady in a long cream dress in the restaurant area in Blenheim, and these too have been linked to Fair Rosamund.

6

University Spirits

I know nothing of the personality of Archbishop Laud, but since he was Chancellor of the University and Archbishop of Canterbury in the 17th century, one visualises a personage of great dignity as befits such high office. However, as a ghost Archbishop Laud shows a refreshingly high spirited style. Beheaded at the Tower of London in 1645 for his support of the Church against Parliament, he was buried beneath the altar of the chapel at **St John's College** in 1663, after an earlier interment in the church of All Hallows, Barking. He favours the library, where he merrily bowls his head along the floor, a disturbing sight for anyone unlucky enough to witness it. He is also said to appear to be cut off at the knees, because the library floor has been raised since his day.

The martyrdom of other bishops is commemorated at the junction of Oxford's **George Street and St Giles** by a large cross of granite and brick inlaid in the street. It commemorates Thomas Cranmer, Archbishop of Canterbury (died 21st March 1556), Hugh Latimer, Bishop of Worcester, and Nicholas Ridley, Bishop of London (who both died on 16th October 1555); all were burnt at the stake at that spot for heresy in the days of Bloody Mary.

It is said that a vision of a phantom pyre has been seen by many people at this place, and in 1995 a young girl of 12 who was on the Oxford Ghost Walk looked back at the memorial and saw a ghostly re-enactment of a burning on that spot in Tudor times. She was even able to describe seeing bags of gunpowder tied round the martyrs' necks, a detail she could hardly have known previously.

Another ghost seen apparently walking round on his knees is Colonel Francis Winderbank at **Merton College**, where, as at St John's College, the floor has been raised. He is also seen in the Fellows' Garden, where he was said to have been shot in 1645 after surrendering to Oliver Cromwell.

Queens College has a more recent apparition in Cuthbert Shields, the name adopted by a clergyman who believed he was the reincarnation of St Cuthbert. When he died he left a collection of his papers to the college, with the provision that they were only to be examined 50 years after his death. When this period had elapsed, the box was opened to reveal an uninteresting collection of dull correspondence, religious tracts, etc., which the librarian left lying on his desk. A colleague who came into the library late that night was surprised to see an unknown clergyman, in old-fashioned clothes, apparently studying the papers, and the same figure has been seen in the upper library on subsequent occasions.

At **Magdalen College** there have been reports of a silent black-clad figure walking across the lawn towards the colonnade arches. It appears to be headless, gliding silently along and disappearing when it reaches the staircase. One eye witness reported, 'Its clothes did not move and it made no sound at all.' Another witness described the apparition as 'a black silhouette keeping pace with me'. There was no sound of footsteps and the figure suddenly disappeared on reaching the colonnade. A house owned by Magdalen College and leased to various occupants was once owned by George Napier, a Jesuit, whose ghost has been seen peering through a third floor bedroom window. The occupants often heard footsteps in the house and on the stairs when no one was there. George Napier was captured in 1568 and executed; his quartered body was displayed on the four gates of Oxford city, with his head on **Christ Church**. It is said that his family secretly collected his remains for burial, except for the head, for which his ghost endlessly searches up and down Banbury Road.

Another story has him driving in a coach and four from Temple Farm to Oxford, not a welcome sight, as anyone who sees him is said to die within a year.

At **University College** Room 1 on Staircase 8 is said to be haunted by Obadiah Walker, who was Master of the College in the reign of James II. Obadiah tried to follow the King when he fled to France, but he was caught and imprisoned. He was freed for the final ten years of his life, but his forlorn spirit still sadly haunts his old college.

St Giles' Churchyard is haunted by the apparition of a grey lady whose legacy, which she intended for the parish charities, was never received. It is thought that her relatives got their hands on the money before the executors could carry out her wishes.

At **Exeter College** the tomb of John Crocker is found in the chapel, where the headless spectre of this Elizabethan scholar appears gaily dressed in a yellow jacket, gown and brown breeches.

Wadham College was built on the site of an Augustinian friary, which no doubt accounts for the fact that it is haunted by a monk. He is said to walk from the chapel and up the steps into the hall. In the 1960s the then head porter was doing his usual security check late at night. He had just left the hall and was en route towards Staircase 4 when on looking towards the chapel doors he saw a white cowled figure, which was quite tall and seemed to be looking at him. Although it seemed what he described as 'a little cloudy', he was not afraid. He moved on to Staircase 5, and when he looked back again he found that the figure was no longer there.

A few years later, in 1967, another scout was clearing up after dinner at high table in Wadham, and as he was leaving the hall he noticed a cowled grey figure by the fireplace. He said it was about six feet tall and looked like a priest, and it was also seen by three other scouts who were working with him. Seconds later the figure had vanished. Other members of staff have had similar experiences and have also heard footsteps in the hall, sometimes from a room below, but on investigation there is never anyone there to account for them.

Miss Eleanor Jourdain, Vice-Principal and later Principal of **St Hugh's College**, will always be associated with her experiences in 1901, when she visited Versailles with her friend Miss Charlotte Moberly and they apparently witnessed people and events there as they were in the 1700s, described in their book *An Adventure*.

These were not Miss Jourdain's only psychic insights. While at Oxford she had several visions of the city's past, including one particularly harrowing one of a pageant of medieval people taking a doomed victim down St Margaret's Road towards the gallows while those watching danced and jeered.

In his book *Holy Ghostbuster*, J. Aelwyn Roberts gives an account of a friend's strange experience when he left his Welsh home for the first time to take up his state scholarship at Oxford when he was 18. The name of the college is not given, but Peter, the new student, was directed by a scout up a narrow stone staircase to Room 16. The door opened to a tiny living room with a small fireplace, in which a good fire was burning. There was a sink with a cold water tap, and an even smaller bedroom beyond, conditions today's undergraduates would find primitive indeed.

Peter looked out of his window at the quad below, where he could see other students walking and talking, and he felt very lonely and homesick. The quad soon became quiet and empty, which Peter found strange, as he had heard about wild all-night parties and other lively activities and it was only 11.30 pm, but he went to bed in his chilly room and tried to sleep.

He had dozed off, when suddenly he became wide awake at the sound of high pitched, excited voices shouting outside, and the light of torches illuminated his bedroom window. The sound of feet and loud voices came from the stairs, and he realised that someone was trying to unlock the door of his living room. Then they must have put their shoulder to it and he heard the wood splintering and the door crashing to the floor. He heard someone say 'Good Gawd, who's got a knife? Who's going to cut him down?' and then, 'Get him, Andrew! Hold him by the legs.'

Peter came to the conclusion that this must be the sort of freshman's rag he had been warned about, but he hadn't thought it would be like this. It was supposed to be fun. His father had said, 'Students tend to lark about with freshmen you know, Peter. Just take it in a good spirit, boy.' But this didn't sound much like larking. Nervously Peter opened his bedroom door to meet whatever was in store, but when he stepped into the other room, incredibly, it was empty, perfectly still and undisturbed. The door was undamaged and locked, as he had left it, and he opened it and stepped out on to the landing. All he could hear was the faint sound of music, probably the sound of the radio in the porter's office down below.

Next morning at breakfast one of the dons casually asked 'Slept well?' and on impulse Peter told him what had happened the night before, insisting that it wasn't a dream. He had been fully awake. The don listened politely, nodding occasionally, then asked, 'What is your room number?'

'Number 16,' said Peter.

'Ah, there lies the explanation, my boy,' was the reply. 'There have been two suicides in Room 16. Both were hangings. One was in the 1850s and the other, if I remember correctly, around 1908. That explains it all. It was a re-enactment lad, it was the hanging all over again. Interesting, what?'

This experience and Miss Jourdain's visions are instances of time slips when someone unexpectedly finds themselves witnessing some event in the past. Often these are happenings so emotionally powerful that certain circumstances can apparently initiate a replay. Perhaps the student Peter's feelings that night to some extent echoed the misery that caused those previous occupants of his room to take their own lives. But what triggers such a re-enactment? Who knows?

7

Did She Fall Or …?

The tragic death of Amy Robsart is one of history's most intriguing mysteries and the truth of what actually happened is unlikely now to be known. But at the time it was generally accepted that Amy's death was no accident and that her husband, Lord Robert Dudley, was implicated.

At the court of the young Queen Elizabeth the tall strikingly handsome Lord Robert had set tongues wagging with rumour and gossip about his relationship with the Queen. As a young unmarried woman the question of Elizabeth's future husband was of much concern to her ministers and ambassadors but despite a steady stream of possible suitors, Elizabeth herself could not be hurried. When the House of Commons in 1559 urged her to consider marriage she replied that she had chosen the virgin life, and yet she confessed that she was but human and her heart and mind might change, and she would do as God directed her.

And so possible suitors came and went while the Queen prevaricated, but it had become obvious that she found one member of her entourage extremely attractive. He was Robert Dudley, dark, handsome and charming, whom she had appointed as her Master of the Horse, which gave him a lodging at court, and Elizabeth's obvious delight in his company was increasingly the subject of rumour and gossip. There were fears that her fondness for Dudley was damaging her reputation and there were even scandalous suggestions that the Queen was pregnant or had actually had a child by Dudley. He was, of course, already married and the scandal-mongers whispered that Dudley intended to get rid of his wife so that he could marry the Queen.

Sir William Cecil, her principal Secretary of State, who had told Her Majesty that he hoped God would direct her to procure a father for her children, confided in the Spanish Ambassador that he thought Dudley's intimacy with Elizabeth would be the ruin of the country, as he was convinced that she intended to marry him. He deplored her behaviour and indiscreetly expressed his opinion that Dudley was thinking of killing his wife, the stumbling block to his ambitions. She was said to be ill, but, said Cecil, that was not true; she was quite well and taking good care not to be poisoned! In the light of events which were about to take place, these remarks were significant.

Amy Dudley was living at Cumnor Place, the Oxfordshire home of Robert Dudley's former steward, Anthony Forster. She was the daughter of a rich Norfolk landowner, and she and Dudley were married in 1550 at the Royal Palace of Sheen in Richmond when she was 18, in a splendid ceremony attended by the young King Edward VI and Elizabeth, who had known Dudley in her youth.

For some time the marriage was happy, but they had no children and as her ambitious husband spent more and more time at court, Amy was neglected and lonely. Gossip about Robert and the Queen must have caused her distress and one of her maids said that she had heard her mistress 'pray to God to deliver her from desperation'. There is also reason to suppose that reports of her ill health may have been true and she may have been suffering from breast cancer.

On Sunday 8th September 1560 Amy sent off her servants to Abingdon Fair, and when they returned they found her dead at the foot of the hall staircase, her neck broken. According to some other ladies staying at Cumnor Place, they had all been playing backgammon when Amy had left the room, and had apparently fallen down the stairs. Word was immediately sent to Robert Dudley, who was with the Queen at Windsor, and he demanded full enquiries 'considering what the malicious world will bruit'. How right he was, as stories that Amy had committed suicide or that her husband was implicated in her death continued to circulate, despite the inquest verdict of accidental death. The Spanish Ambassador was heard to repeat court gossip that the Queen and Dudley 'were thinking of destroying Lord Robert's wife' and said that four days before Amy Dudley's fatal accident the Queen had told him that Lord Robert's wife was dead, or nearly so, and begged him to say nothing about it.

The English Ambassador in Paris also reported that it was the general opinion that Lady Dudley had been murdered and her husband was responsible.

Dudley arranged a handsome funeral for his wife, but did not attend himself. Meanwhile suspicion focused on him was strengthened when it was reported that Amy's ghost had been seen on the staircase at Cumnor Place, where she continued to haunt for many years even after the Elizabethan house had been replaced. It is said that the ghost was laid by twelve clergymen in a pool afterwards known as Lady Dudley's Pond, and from that day onwards the pond never froze. But the exorcism cannot have been entirely successful, as Amy's ghost continued to be seen elsewhere.

Despite the scandalous rumours about his wife's mysterious accident, the Queen had complete faith in Dudley's innocence. But, although Dudley remained in favour, and in 1564 was created Earl of Leicester, and despite her infatuation, Elizabeth realised that Amy Robsart's death had left a cloud on his reputation which eliminated the possibility of their marriage. The question of a husband for Elizabeth would continue for many years, but as she said more than once, 'I am already bound unto a husband which is the Kingdom of England.'

However, the depth of her feelings for Dudley may be judged by her reaction when some years later she discovered that he had secretly married her cousin, Lettice Knollys, the widowed Countess of Essex. Elizabeth was incandescent with rage and immediately demanded that he should be arrested and sent to the Tower! With difficulty she was calmed down and convinced that he was perfectly free to marry and had done nothing wrong. Dudley restored the situation by sending word that he was ill, which brought the Queen anxiously hurrying to his bedside, and all was well. He was allowed to return to court when he had recovered, but not with his wife.

In 1588, when Elizabeth's affections had turned to his stepson, the Earl of Essex, Dudley died suddenly at Cornbury Park in Oxfordshire. It's said that he was hunting in Wychwood Forest when he encountered the spirit of Amy Robsart, who declared: 'In ten days thou will be with me.'

Back at the house he suddenly became seriously ill and died, and since then the ghost of Amy Robsart has continued to haunt the area, her appearance being considered a death warning to anyone who meets her at nightfall.

8

Ghost in a Birdcage

It was in the 1970s that I first visited the Birdcage pub, one of the oldest and most picturesque buildings in Thame, part of it dating back to the late 13th century. I was writing a series of true ghost stories for a women's magazine at the time, and when a group of psychic investigators I knew told me about the paranormal happenings at the Birdcage, I arranged to visit it as soon as possible.

Mrs Pat Ellis, the landlady, and her husband had been running the pub for about five years, and it was quite soon after they arrived that Pat had her first inkling that there was something uncanny about the place. 'I first discovered there was an eerie sort of atmosphere in the middle of the night, about two months after we came here,' she told me. 'I came downstairs one night about half past two feeling thirsty, and thought I'd get a bitter lemon from the bar. You have to walk to the centre of the public bar to reach the light switches, and I was almost there when suddenly I felt really frightened. I didn't know why, but I didn't stop to get the drink, I just dashed back upstairs.

'After that I started waking up at about half past two night after night, and just couldn't get to sleep again. Then I heard the footsteps.' Pat showed me how the second stair going up from the bar creaks when trodden on.

'I would hear it creak,' she said, 'and then the sound of somebody coming upstairs. Then as soon as the footsteps reached the top of the house, there'd be a terribly loud, demanding knock.'

Sometimes the knocking would go on for about an hour on and off, but Pat noticed that it always stopped at 4 am. At first she told herself that she must be imagining things. She had never had any previous paranormal experiences, and no one had said anything about the Birdcage being haunted.

Pat's husband was a sound sleeper, but to satisfy his wife he did get up and have a look round, but there was never anything to see. Pat's young son's room was also on the top floor, and when she asked if he ever heard knocking in the night, he replied cheerfully, 'Oh yes, sometimes. I just knock back and it stops.'

The Birdcage wasn't always an inn. It probably started out as a market house, used to control and administer the market, and there have been various additions to the building over the years. In the 16th century documents referred to it as 'a tenement called The Cage', and around 1600 it was held as copyhold by a yeoman called Philip Bird, which suggests that this was when it became known as Bird's Cage, later the Birdcage. I was told that there is a tradition that the top floor was where lepers were kept at one time, shut away and shunned by their fellow citizens, their food being hoisted up to them on a long pole.

As time went on Pat Ellis had more evidence of the presence of the restless spirit that was haunting the pub. One night she was in the bar talking to a regular customer, who told her frankly that in his opinion the stories about the ghost were some kind of publicity stunt. Unknown to Pat, three girls also in the bar were watching fascinated as a silver tankard, hanging from the oak beam above her head, started to swing backwards and forwards. Then suddenly it became unhooked and rose up in the air, dropping suddenly to give Pat a sharp blow on the back of her neck. 'It's funny,' she told me, 'but if we talk about the ghost, and somebody takes the mickey, something nearly always happens.' She also told me about the time when a conversation about ghosts was going on in the bar. Suddenly the large heavy till slid off the counter and crashed down at the back of the bar.

Pat's son and her daughter, who both slept on the upper floor, complained about being disturbed in the night, with the feeling that someone had come into their rooms. And a visitor who also had a room at the top said that he hadn't had a wink of sleep as his clothes on metal hangers in the wardrobe had been moving about noisily all night. When a film was being made in Thame two cameramen stayed at the Birdcage in a twin bedded room. Next morning one said to Pat, 'Did you know you've got a ghost up there?' He described seeing 'a sort of cold mist drifting out of the door', while his friend who had seen nothing laughed at him. But next morning he, too, came down in a subdued frame of mind and said, 'It's true, you have got a ghost.'

Pat found that the various uncanny happenings were preying on her mind, and when a group of psychic investigators offered to see if they could help, she readily agreed to let them try.

The group's leader told me afterwards what happened. The four men and two women settled down in the most haunted bedroom at about midnight, and at first nothing happened. Then, just after 2 am, they heard sounds of footsteps on the stairs, and then a noise on the top landing. The group's leader opened the bedroom door and shone his torch, but there was nothing to see. He went back into the room, and almost at once the handle of the door began to rattle.

'The door didn't open,' he said, 'but suddenly there were sounds inside the room with us, and knocking on the floor and walls. I was conscious of the most depressing sensation I ever remember, and I felt deeply disturbed.' The group sat, hands touching, round a small table, and using the method of one rap for Yes and two raps for No, they began to get a response. The leader also repeated the letters of the alphabet, asking for a rap after each correct letter, and slowly built up words. They all listened, tense in the darkness as the first message slowly came.

'Kill you.'

'Do you mean us?'

'Yes!'

'I explained we wanted to help him find peace', said the leader, 'and asked why he was there.'

'I am a leper, and was stoned to death,' came the reply. Then the words became more menacing. 'Go now,' was rapped out. 'Go! Go!'

By now the atmosphere was frighteningly oppressive, and after a prayer the group were very glad to leave.

Then one day Pat decided to try talking to the ghost herself. She had begun to feel more pity than fear for this unhappy lost soul. 'I felt an absolute fool,' she told me, 'but I went into the haunted room and said, "Look here, old boy, if you really want to stay, I don't mind so long as you stop frightening the life out of my children and my guests. I really feel sorry for you."'

Just then she felt a push at the back of her legs, and nearly fainted with fright. But it was only her dog which had followed her up the stairs! After that, the knocking in the night quietened down, and Pat was quite relaxed as she showed me round the inn. We ended up in the whitewashed cellar, where she pointed out some old pieces of iron embedded in the walls, probably a legacy of the days when chains and shackles were used for prisoners. It is known that prisoners were kept there during the Napoleonic Wars, and I thought the place had a sad, oppressive feeling. When Pat whispered, 'I just can't bear this place,' I knew what she meant.

I had not visited the Birdcage again until the autumn of 2002, while researching this book, and was curious to know if it was still haunted. The young couple now running the pub assured me that it definitely still had a ghost, but there is nothing of the hostile spirit of the leper there today. They told me that they do hear noises, especially upstairs, and mentioned odd scratching sounds, but laughed as they pointed out that there are always pigeons on the roof. They call their ghost Pete, and when I asked if Pete is ever seen they said that sometimes you can notice something moving out of the corner of your eye, but when you look round there is nothing there. There is a large old-fashioned mirror in the bar, and sometimes they have noticed a shadowy, undefined reflection that disappears on closer inspection, and there are unexplained cold spots.

So it appears that the new ghost in the Birdcage is very different from the hostile spirit of Pat Ellis's time. It is a happy, bustling establishment, and he is a friendly personality, whom they say is very welcome there.

9

❖❖❖❖❖❖❖❖❖❖❖❖❖❖❖❖❖❖

Shades of the Prison House

Oxford

Oxford's former prison by the Castle Mound was decommissioned in 1997 and bought by the county council, it's said for the astonishingly cheap price of £9,000! Afterwards among the city's many delights there have been occasional Heritage Days with the possibility of touring the building and imagining what it must have been like to share one of the cramped cells with their small half-moon windows, intended for one inmate, but often used for three – prison overcrowding is nothing new.

One council enterprise was to allow the prison to be used by film and television companies, and some episodes of *Inspector Morse* and *The Bill* were shot there.

An old prison is bound to be a place where misery and despair have left their mark on the atmosphere. The last public hanging took place on the roof in 1863, but other executions continued until the 1950s inside the prison. So not surprisingly, there are ghost stories.

Even when the prison was in use the place had acquired a reputation for being more than a little scary. In the 1970s some of the inmates in the modern block decided to hold an impromptu séance, which apparently had the undesirable result of starting an outbreak of poltergeist activity. Two guards on duty one night were alarmed to see a white misty shape drifting up a flight of steps towards them, and even more alarmed as it came nearer only to vanish in front of them.

But a guard and his dog patrolling the prison on another occasion had an even more chilling experience. As they walked along, the dog suddenly paused and began to growl menacingly, and the guard saw two strange figures ahead. They appeared to be black shapes with no visible arms or legs, and before the guard could call out to challenge them they turned towards him only to fade away before his eyes. His dog seemed to have been so badly frightened by the apparitions that it died a few days later.

During the time when the prison was used by film companies there were various reports of hearing unexplained voices coming from the former cells, and sometimes sounds of shouting or even screams. And film crews sometimes found that equipment had been tampered with when no one was around.

Cleaning staff, too, often working alone in the buildings, reported hearing a voice yelling 'Help, let me out!' from an empty cell. One cleaner was startled when she saw a bucket suddenly began to spin round by itself, and, when, not unnaturally frightened, she ran outside, a plastic bin bag rose up in front of her and whirled round in the air.

Abingdon

The Old Gaol in Abingdon dates back to the time of the Napoleonic Wars, and it became a grain store for a time after its closure in 1890. Later, when it became a sports centre, there were reports of sightings of shadowy figures and echoes of mysterious voices, and sometimes doors would bang for no apparent reason.

When the sports centre took over the building, the health suite was built on the site of the former prison chapel, where many a condemned man was given the last rites before his encounter with the hangman, and this was no place for those of a nervous disposition. But a deputy manager there insisted that the ghosts, which seemed at their most active when the building work was being done, were really quite harmless. But he did admit that he had never encountered anything supernatural himself!

One of the most touching stories refers to the sound of a child's voice which staff heard laughing and talking at closing time. This has been associated with the claim that the youngest child to be hanged in Britain met his end at Abingdon. His crime apparently was that he had 'malice, cunning and revenge in firing two barns'.

I have tried without success to verify the facts of this tragic story. In *The History of Judicial Hanging in Britain*, the youngest child hanging ever recorded was given as that of Michael Hammond, aged 7, hung with his sister, aged 11, at Kings Lynn in 1808. *The Guinness Book of Records* gives the youngest child hanging ever recorded as that of a 7 year old girl, also in 1808 at Lynn, so it seems likely that these both refer to the same disturbing event, inaccurately reported in one case.

10

❖◆❖◆❖◆❖◆❖◆❖◆❖◆❖◆❖◆❖◆❖◆❖◆❖

A Devil at Woodstock

Today there is nothing left of Woodstock Palace except memories, a small stone monument (see Chapter 5), and a rather curious tale about a poltergeist.

From earliest times there was a huge forest at Woodstock, which became a royal hunting ground, and during his reign from 1100–1135 William the Conqueror's son Henry I built a hunting lodge there. He also brought to Woodstock more exotic animals than the local wildlife, keeping lions, leopards and camels in a large-walled enclosure.

Over the years a village with a manor house developed, each subsequent king adding to what became a grand palace with a thriving town by the middle of the 15th century. Henry VII's contribution was to bring water in wooden pipes to provide baths and a splendid fountain in the courtyard, and Henry VIII built a tennis court, but not long afterwards the palace fell into disrepair and needed 'tyling and glasyng' before Queen Mary chose Woodstock as one of the great houses where she imprisoned her sister Elizabeth in 1554. When she became Queen, Elizabeth encouraged the prosperity of Woodstock, where the industries of glove making and steelwork flourished, but by the time of the Civil War, Woodstock's fortunes again took a downturn.

Woodstock Palace was under siege in April 1646 and finally taken by Cromwell's forces. It was sometime later in 1649 that parliamentary commissioners arrived there, making themselves comfortable in what had been King Charles's own rooms, and using his bedchamber as a kitchen. They demolished the huge old tree known as the King's Oak in the park, storing the wood in the dining room, and committed many acts of mindless vandalism. It seems fanciful to imagine that this disrespectful behaviour aroused the fury of a spirit with Royalist sympathies, but soon afterwards on 16th October 1685 the commissioners and their servants found themselves under some kind of paranormal attack.

They noticed what seemed to be a dog which came into their bedroom and started gnawing underneath the beds, accompanied by terrifying growls. Another night the beds were hoisted up and down so violently by some unseen force that the occupants were badly bruised. The King's Oak wood was found strewn about the dining room and furniture was overturned. Ghostly footsteps sounded in the bedchamber, followed alarmingly by unseen presences hurling logs of wood. Bricks were mysteriously dislodged from the chimney to whirl around the heads of the frightened commissioners. But this was only the beginning. Stones, bones, trenchers and glass were thrown about, fires and candles were extinguished as soon as they were lit, and bedding and curtains were ripped up. Once a warming pan crashed down on the table followed by a heavy shower of stones. The servants were drenched with 'stinking ditch water', and although no windows were broken they were pelted with broken glass.

October 29th brought new terrors when the walls shook and windows were smashed to thunderous noises which could be heard outside the building, and this happened several times to the alarm of villagers, not to mention the beleaguered occupants of Woodstock Palace. One of the Roundheads saw what appeared to be a hoof kicking out a candle but when he tried to strike it with his sword the weapon was snatched from him by an invisible hand and he was knocked down and stunned.

This was the final straw for the commissioners and their servants, and they all left, defeated by their invisible opponent – and that was the last anyone ever heard of the Royalist Devil of Woodstock.

So was their tormentor a poltergeist of strong Royalist sympathies? There is reason to suspect that the Clerk to the Commissioners, one Giles Sharp (real name Joseph Collins), was a secret Royalist who may have been more au fait with the Royalist Devil's activities than anyone imagined. He knew every inch of the Palace of Woodstock like the back of his hand, and with his awareness of all its secret hiding places, cupboards, chimneys and trapdoors, it is not inconceivable that he could have masterminded the poltergeist reign of terror that turned Cromwell's commissioners' attempts to vandalise Woodstock into a rout.

11

Wartime Memories

Many old wartime airfields have a history of strange happenings – the sound of a plane in an empty sky, a man in uniform who casually walks through a solid wall, or an apparently normal serviceman who hitches a lift, only to disappear en route. With so many airfields from which RAF and USAAF bombers and fighter planes flew out on their dangerous missions, perhaps it is not surprising that so much courage and cameraderie coupled with tragedy and loss has left more than memories.

Grove airfield near Wantage opened in 1943 and the US Air Force were there from 1944 until 1946. Afterwards it returned to the RAF to be used as a relief landing ground until 1954, when it was eventually sold. It was in the late 1970s that the old airfield was used by the Metal Box Company for their research and development complex, and it wasn't long before there were rumours that the area at the rear of the works was haunted. People spoke of being aware of a presence, and then the ghostly figure of an airman in flying kit and wearing an oxygen mask was seen near the old chapel and the officers' mess.

Naturally these reports caused great interest among the employees and reached the local press, and theories were put forward to account for the haunting. One suggestion was that the ghost could be a fighter pilot whose plane had crashed on landing at Grove airfield in 1945, and he had been burnt to death.

Another possibility was that the ghostly airman was a local man called Symons. His Lancaster bomber was on a bombing mission to Germany when soon after take-off its engine failed, necessitating an emergency landing at Grove airfield. But the plane crashed on landing, exploding its bombs, and all the crew were killed. To add to the tragedy, Symons's father who worked at Clarke's Mill, had seen the Lancaster flying low and obviously in trouble before it crashed at Grove.

Before the Metal Box Company moved into Grove airfield, there had been reports of something strange about the area. An old aircraft hangar was used by the Atomic Energy Authority for operating an irradiation plant. This ran day and night, and one evening in 1969 at about 9 pm a man in the office was surprised to hear voices outside, as he knew there should be no one there.

The duty officer made a recce outside and found the hangar quite empty, and after looking round he telephoned the security officer at the gatehouse, who reported that apart from the two of them, and a boilerman who was with him at the time, no one else was on the site. The duty officer mentioned this curious happening to his colleagues later, but most people thought it was either the noise of the plant working, or his imagination.

But a month later, when the same duty officer was working one evening, he again heard the sound of voices outside his office, and this time there was no question of its being caused by the plant, which was out of order and quite silent at the time. The duty officer went outside and looked round the hangar, but as before, there was no one there.

Some time later one of his colleagues confirmed that he, too, had heard the same murmur of voices from an empty hangar. And they learnt that during the war an American serviceman had hanged himself in that same hangar.

Another curious story concerns Culham, which opened in 1944 as a centre for naval reservists and after the war was used to house the staff of No. 1 Parachute Training School, Parachute Regiment and RAF personnel, who had their meals at Culham after their day's training at RAF Abingdon.

One night in June 1959 a man called Brian Leigh was disturbed in the night by the sound of a heavy thunderstorm. He was sleeping in an old Nissan hut and when he opened his eyes he noticed the glow of the old-fashioned stove which heated the hut. But as he became more awake, he realised that this was odd since the stove was not, of course, in use in summertime.

He sat up in bed and was amazed to see five Royal Navy men sitting round the stove. 'They were all in their best uniforms,' he said, 'and all were bandaged either on their arms, hands or head.' He noticed, too, that one man looked very boyish, but judging from his uniform was obviously an officer.

Brian gazed at this unexpected sight with disbelief. The men were quite close to him and clearly visible and were taking no notice of him. After a few seconds he let out a shout, and immediately the men vanished. He leapt out of bed and rushed towards the stove, which he now found was not alight and felt completely cold. He woke his companions in the hut, and they sat around discussing the strange happening – naturally his leg was pulled, but his story had made sufficient impression for some of the men to refuse to sleep in that particular hut afterwards.

12

Magic and Mysteries

The Oxfordshire countryside still bears many traces of its ancient past. It is crossed by the prehistoric tracks of the Ridgeway and the Icknield Way which pass near to that most graceful and elegantly simple figure cut in the chalk hillside, the Uffington White Horse.

The Icknield Way, said to be haunted by Roman legionaries and black dogs, was at one time believed to lead directly to hell. On the Ridgeway about half a mile away is a Neolithic long barrow known as Wayland's Smithy, and between Great and Little Rollright you can find one of the most mysterious stone circles, a place of folklore, magic, witchcraft and fairies.

The white horse, approximately 365 ft long, is thought to date from the early Iron Age, like nearby Uffington Castle, where a large fair used to be held every seven years for the ritual scouring of the hill figure's outline. This was a lively event for general fun and games, horse racing, wrestling and a race for a large cheese as it bowled down the steep hillside to a combe below the white horse, known as the 'Manger'. These fairs continued until 1857, after which the horse was only cleaned occasionally.

The flat-topped hill below the figure is known as Dragon Hill and traditionally believed to be where Saint George killed and buried the dragon. The bare chalk area there where no grass grows is said to have been poisoned by the dragon's blood. Some believe that the Uffington White Horse is in fact intended to represent a dragon! Another idea is that the figure depicts the white mare goddess Rhiannon, who was known as Epona to the Romans, an agricultural goddess worshipped as the spirit of the land.

The horse figure is also associated with Wayland's Smithy. According to legend Wayland Smith was an invisible blacksmith and if a traveller's horse had lost a shoe, he was advised to tether his animal near Wayland's cave and leave a coin on the anvil in payment, and when he returned he would find the horse had been shod. In Sir Walter Scott's *Kenilworth*, he writes: 'Here lived a supernatural smith, who would shoe a traveller's horse for a "consideration". His fee was sixpence, and if more was offered him he was offended.'

The White Horse of Uffington is said to leave its place on the hillside once a century to be shod at Wayland's Smithy. There is a story that the last time this happened, around a hundred years ago, a stranger entered an inn below the hill. He had an old-fashioned appearance with a tall hat and leather apron, and while he was sitting drinking suddenly those in the inn heard the sound of a horn outside. At that the newcomer leapt to his feet and rushed away, and the sound of galloping hooves was heard. Everyone in the inn ran outside, where the sound of horse's hooves was deafening, apparently coming from overhead.

To their astonishment, as the sound faded away towards Wayland's Smithy, they noticed that the familiar outline of the chalk horse had disappeared from the hill, to return just as mysteriously later. Those who experienced this uncanny event believed that the stranger in the pub had been Wayland himself, summoned for the ritual shoeing of the white horse!

Perhaps it is not surprising that horses are involved in many of the supernatural manifestations in the area.

Near Wantage is the Letcombe Brook where at times of national danger the water becomes wild and turbulent, churned up by the hooves of hundreds of invisible horses apparently crossing over the stream. This strange happening was seen at the time of both the Boer War and the First World War.

And at Charlbury, drivers are advised to keep a wary eye while driving on the B4022 for a huge white stallion which has been known to leap over the hedge and charge across the road in front of the traffic. One motorist once saw it clear a hedge which topped a seven foot high embankment. As I mention in Chapter 2, there is also a phantom coach and horses that is sometimes seen on the road from Charlbury to Finstock. At times only the sound of horses hooves and the rumbling of an invisible carriage are heard, and then they become visible as they disappear round a bend in the road in the direction of Finstock.

It is a common tradition that the stones of many ancient circles were once human beings, who were petrified for dancing or doing something they shouldn't on the Sabbath. But the Rollright Stone Circle's story is a different one. It was first printed by Camden in 1586, and relates how a king and his men, bent on the conquest of England, were accosted by a witch when they arrived at the site of the Rollrights. She challenged the king with these words:

'Seven long strides shalt thou take,
  And if Long Compton thou canst see,
  King of England thou shalt be.'

Striding off, the king shouted: 'Stick, stock, stone,
  As King of England I shall be known.'

But so much for his ambitions, as he reached his seventh stride, the witch caused a mound of earth to rise up obscuring his view, and laughing at the disappointed monarch, she cried:

'As Long Compton thou canst not see,
  King of England thou shalt not be.
  Rise up stick and stand still stone,
  For King of England thou shalt be none.
  Thou and thy men hoar stones shall be,
  And I myself an eldern tree.'

The king then became the King Stone and his men the King's Men Stone Circle, and his knights were turned into the small group of five stones 400 yards away from the circle, known as the Whispering Knights. Legend has it that at midnight on New Year's Eve the king's men come back to life and go down to a nearby stream to drink and dance. Anyone witnessing this amazing sight is in danger of going mad or dying, an alarming prediction that may have originated to keep inquisitive villagers away from witches' ceremonies at the site. Its an old belief that the stones cannot be counted or taken away, but should anyone count them three times and come up with the same total, they will get their heart's desire!

Apparently a farmer once took the capstone of the Whispering Knights, which are the remains of a Neolithic dolmen, to build a bridge across a stream. It took several heavy horses to drag the stone downhill, but once there the farmer was so troubled by strange frightening noises that he decided to return it. And this time only one horse was needed to return the stone to its place.

Fairies are said to live beneath the King Stone, and come out to dance at midnight. There is a long tradition of witchcraft associated with the stones and their mysterious power, and pagan ceremonies are still held there. Its said that the Whispering Knights can foretell the future, and in past times young girls would put their ears to the stones hoping to hear the name of their future husband. The King Stone was supposed to be able to promote fertility, and young women wishing for a child would visit it at night to touch it with their breasts. People have often chipped off pieces of the stones for a good luck charm, although damaging them has sometimes had the opposite effect.

Since the late 1970s the Rollright Stones have been the focus of the Dragon Project, formed to investigate and identify the earth energies emanating from them. Read Don Robins' book *Circles of Silence* for further information on this study, and on this enduringly fascinating place of secrets and mysteries.

13

Purposeful Ghosts

Ghosts come in many guises and although few actually communicate verbally with the living, there are some who return with a purpose or to give a warning, such as the ghost of Herne the Hunter, said to haunt Windsor Great Park, and to appear whenever disaster threatens the Royal Family or the nation.

The ghost of Amy Robsart (see Chapter 7) appeared to her unfaithful husband, the Earl of Leicester, when he was hunting in Wychwood Forest with the words: 'In ten days thou will be with me.' This dire warning proved to be true, as before ten days had passed he was dead. Her ghost is also said to be a warning of sudden death to anyone who meets her.

A Ghost with a Warning

There is a stone in the chancel of Souldern village church which reads:

> Here lies the body of Jeffry Shaw B.D.
> Rector of this Church
> Who Fell down Dead While He Was
> Reading Divine Service Therein
> On Sunday Nov XVII MDCCVI
> Blessed Is That Servant Whom His Lord
> When He Cometh Shall Find So Doing.

The story behind this happening is an unusual and interesting one. One summer evening, 28th July 1706, the Revd Jeffry

Shaw was sitting reading in his study when he was interrupted by the unannounced arrival of a visitor. It was an old friend of his, Master Nailor, the former Vicar of Enstone, whose appearance was all the more unexpected as he had died two years previously.

With admirable calm the Revd Shaw invited his friend to be seated and listened as Master Nailor explained the purpose of his visit. He said that a mutual friend of theirs, Mr Orchard, was about to die suddenly, and even more to the point, his listener, Jeffry Shaw, would soon be leaving this life for the next.

The Revd Shaw's reaction to this alarming news is unknown, but he took the opportunity of questioning his visitant from the next world about the afterlife. Master Nailor was disappointingly uncommunicative about that, although he said that he was well and happy, but had not apparently made contact with other old friends who had passed on. However, he did explain that he had been allowed just three days 'leave of absence' and his time was now up and so he departed.

As recounted in *The Gentleman's Magazine*, their friend Arthur Orchard ended his days soon afterwards, as the ghost had predicted, followed by the Revd Jeffry Shaw, who died suddenly of apoplexy as he was reading the lesson at evening service.

Who Will Look After My Clocks?

Another clerical gentleman who apparently returned with a purpose was the Vicar of Deddington, the Revd Maurice Frost, who departed this life on Christmas Day 1961. But it was not long before his cousin, Mr H. Campbell Jarrett, who had come over from Italy to deal with the Revd Frost's affairs, realised that something rather strange was happening. In April 1962 it was reported that when Mr Jarrett was about to wind up his cousin's collection of antique clocks, the winding handle was taken out of his hand, and he believed that his cousin's ghost had returned to take care of them. In the mornings the beds were found pressed down as if someone had slept in them, and a familiar cough was heard in the drawing room and noises in the study when no one was there. One of the maids assumed it must have been Mr Jarrett but when she went upstairs she found him in his bedroom.

The staff were so alarmed by the strange happenings that they refused to stay, so eventually the clock collection was removed from the vicarage in the hope that the ghost of the Revd Frost would go with them.

A Ghost with a Message

At Ipsden there is an unusual memorial. It is hard to find and overgrown and neglected, but if you persevere in your search you will see a white stone monument rising to a pyramid and surrounded by railings; on it is the following inscription:

John Thurlow Reade
Esquire
Sehaarunpore
November 25 AD 1827
'Alas my brother'

Why you may wonder is such a memorial placed in such an out of the way place? There is a story behind it that is unusual in the realm of ghost stories.

John Reade was a member of the family who lived at Ipsden House, and after he left school he joined the East India Company and went to India in 1817. He was devoted to his mother, and wrote to her regularly, and when she knew that one of John's usual letters was due she liked to walk down the hill to the Wallingford road to collect it from the carrier.

So when quite an unusually long period had passed without any communication from her son, John's mother became very worried about him. Something told her that she should go down to the Wallingford road as usual one day, and she would have news of her son. And so she did, but it was not the kind of news she hoped for or could have anticipated.

As she drew near to the place where the memorial stone now stands, she saw an apparition of her son standing there in a state of great distress. She felt sure that he was trying to tell her of his death, and, believing that he may have been buried without Christian rites, she arranged for the vicar to hold a burial service for him at the local church.

It was not long before the East India Company confirmed that her son had indeed died at Sehaarunpore and had been buried where he died by his servants.

And when John Reade's brother Edward became master of Ipsden House he erected the memorial to his brother in 1860, on the spot where their mother had seen John's ghost.

14

Lord Lovell and the Mistletoe Bride

Beside the river Windrush near Burford stand the imposing ruins of Minster Lovell Hall, a place with a strange story and a ghost to go with it. The Lovells were one of the most important families in the land, but after the defeat of Richard III at the Battle of Bosworth in 1485, Francis, Viscount Lovell fled to Flanders. When he returned he threw in his lot with the wrong side by supporting the pretender to the throne, Lambert Simnel. After the Battle of Stoke, when the uprising was defeated, Lord Lovell hurried home to Minster Lovell, where he apparently disappeared. There were various stories about what had happened to him. It was thought possible that he had died on the field of battle. Stories also persisted that he had drowned when he tried to cross the river Trent on horseback. But whatever his fate, Francis Lovell had disappeared, and was never seen again.

The truth was that he had hidden himself in a secret chamber in the Hall, where only one other person, his faithful old servant, knew where he was and kept him supplied with food. But his servant died suddenly, leaving Lovell, locked in his hideaway, to starve.

It was not until 1708 when workmen were restoring the hall that a secret panel was discovered, and inside they found a small cell. There they came across a skeleton sitting at the table, with the skeleton of a dog at his feet. The mystery of

Lord Lovell's disappearance was solved, and almost at once both skeletons crumbled to dust.

There have been sightings of Minster Lovell's ghostly White Knight, a knight in shining armour riding a white horse – is this perhaps Francis Lovell returning from battle to his long incarceration and death?

There is another story of a tragic disappearance associated with Minster Lovell Hall. Most people have heard the story of the Mistletoe Bough, where a young bride on her wedding day was playing hide-and-seek with her new husband and guests. The bride hurried off to hide and, confident that she had discovered the perfect hiding place, she climbed into an old oak chest, but when she closed the lid a spring lock imprisoned her for ever. Her frantic young husband and the guests searched everywhere in growing desperation but she was never found, and it was not until years later that an old chest that had been stored in the attic was opened to reveal its sad secret.

Minster Lovell Hall is one of several places that claim to be the site of the Mistletoe Bough story, and many a handsome old chest has been described as the one where the skeleton of the lovely young bride in her wedding gown was discovered, a sprig of mistletoe beside her. Writer Thomas Haynes Bayley (1797–1839) wrote the ballad *The Mistletoe Bough* inspired by the belief that the tragedy occurred at Marwell Hall, Owslebury in Hampshire, home of the Seymour family. Bramshill House at Hartley Wintney, also in Hampshire, is another old manor house that has been associated with the story of the mistletoe bride. So why is Minster Lovell Hall also considered to be a candidate? Possibly because of the following lines in the ballad:

And young Lovel cried 'O! where dost thou hide?
I am lonely without thee, my own dear bride.'

And the story continues:

At length an old chest that had long laid hid
Was found in the castle – they raised the lid;
A skeleton form lay mouldering there,
In the bridal wreath of that lady fair,
Oh! sad was her fate! In sportive jest
She hid from her lord in that old oak chest.
It closed with a spring, and her bridal bloom
Lay withering there in a living tomb.

The reason why the name of Lovel was used in the ballad for the sorrowing bridegroom is something we may never know. However, in *A Ghost Hunter's Game Book*, James Wentworth Day reveals an interesting possibility. He says that in a village called Bawdrip in Somerset the small church contains a black marble slab behind the altar. This is dedicated to various members of the Lovel family, Edward, his wife Eleanor, and his two daughters Mary and Eleanor, and says that both parents were from a noble family. The mother, Eleanor, died in 1666, Mary in 1675, Edward, who had been rector of the church for fourteen years, died in 1671 and Eleanor, the remaining daughter, in 1681. It is in the reference to the daughter, Eleanor, that there may be a clue. The slab states: 'Her most sorrowing husband mourned her, taken away by a sudden and untimely fate at the very time of the marriage celebrations.'

What can have been the sudden and untimely fate which befell Eleanor on her wedding day? The name of Eleanor's husband is not given so we do not know Eleanor's married name, and have no further information on her mysterious fate. Was she in fact, the mistletoe bride?

The ruins of Minster Lovell are haunted from time to time by a white lady around Christmas time. In September 1993 a local Witney resident and his friend visited the hall one evening and as they walked through the ruins they suddenly saw the white lady, later describing her as a young girl in her teens wearing a long white gown, a wreath of flowers on her long dark hair. She was in what would have been the main chamber and they watched as she mounted invisible stairs and on reaching a height of about fifteen feet she suddenly disappeared.

The chest in which it is claimed the bride was entombed is now at Greys Court, Rotherford Greys, Henley, which once belonged to the Lovell family and these days is a National Trust property. But when I enquired I was told that the white lady has not been seen there.

15

A Grey Lady at Rycote Chapel

Rycote Chapel stands in Rycote Park, a few miles from Thame. It was built in 1449 of local stone by Richard Quatremayne and his wife, Sibil, as the chapel to Rycote's large medieval manor. But now this is all that remains of a historical estate visited by Henry VIII, and by his daughter Elizabeth with a huge entourage, when she became Queen. James I was entertained there and Charles I when his parliament was at Oxford during the plague, and again during the Civil War.

The interior of the chapel is dominated by two extraordinary early 17th century pews, one with a minstrel's gallery, its ceiling charmingly decorated by a blue sky with white clouds and golden stars. During restoration work in the 1960s it was discovered that the stars had been cut from ancient playing cards and gilded before being put in place. The other pew, known as the Royal Pew, is domed and is believed to have been installed before a visit by Charles I in 1625. An unusual item is a fireplace by the north wall of the chapel, the purpose of which can only be guessed, although it may have been used for baking the wafers for mass.

Princess Elizabeth was familiar with Rycote when she was in the charge of Lord John Williams, the owner, whom her sister, Queen Mary, had appointed one of her guardians while she was detained at Woodstock Palace. Elizabeth had found Williams kind and congenial and she was fond of his daughter Marjery, who became a good friend.

When Marjery, now married to Henry Norreys, inherited Rycote, Elizabeth stayed there several times, and in 1566 she arrived for a visit with a splendid retinue, including the Earl of Leicester. It was said that on the fine September morning that the Queen and her court were expected at Rycote, the sound of the horses could be heard there long before the cavalcade came into sight, and when the Queen reached the entrance to Rycote House the end of her entourage was only just turning off the Tetsworth road.

It must have been a splendid sight, and when the Queen and her courtiers were greeted by the Norreys household, she, delighted to be with her old friends, clasped Lady Marjery's hand in hers and held it tight as they listened to Lord Henry's speech of welcome. The Queen had not forgotten the kindness of Marjery and her father in less happy days when her sister Mary was Queen and her own future was uncertain.

According to *The Rycote Yew*, the book about Rycote by former custodian Mr A. Clifford Morris, it was at about the time of another visit by Queen Elizabeth in 1592 that the ghost of a monk was first glimpsed in the stable block of the great house. This ghost has been seen by many people since then right up until more recent times. But the ghost which has inspired the most interest is known locally as the Grey Lady, and often referred to by Mr Morris as Lady Arabella. She was first seen in the 17th century, during a full moon, walking around outside the chapel.

In October 1745 a fire partly destroyed the house, but the chapel escaped unscathed. Only the stable block of the main house remained, eventually to be made into the present house. But the chapel gradually deteriorated to such an extent that at one time it was being used as a store and a cattleshed. In Clifford Morris's book he describes how by the 20th century briars and nettles had covered the chapel walls and farm animals and chickens were causing great damage to the beautiful old woodwork inside. The doors were hanging half off their hinges and there were holes in the roof letting in the weather. In 1952 the chapel was put into the care of the Ministry of Public Building and Works, and, after much needed renovation and restoration had taken place, Rycote Chapel was opened to the public at Easter 1967.

But throughout the chapel's long history, one thing has remained. The famous yew tree on the grass alongside was traditionally planted to mark the coronation of King Stephen in 1135. It is now a huge and magnificent tree, said to have a circumference of about 26 ft.

It seems only right and proper that Mr Morris, with his great love and appreciation for the unique chapel of which he was custodian for many years, should have been given the opportunity to see Rycote's famous ghost, the Grey Lady. It happened at 3.55 pm on 1st December 1968, and in his own words: 'She appeared near to the 800 year old yew tree, and my first impression was that she was one of the ladies from Rycote House in fancy dress. She was tall and slim and was indeed of a pale grey colour with a kind of sheen, something like satin.'

When Mr Morris walked towards the yew tree the lady had disappeared, but as he looked across the lawn on the south side of the chapel, there she was again, standing near his office. 'As I watched her,' he said, 'she moved across the grass and passed behind the east end of the chapel.' She glided along the original route from the site of the house to the chapel and as she reached the level lawn at the bottom of a slope beneath a chestnut tree, the lady vanished.

Mr Morris realised that his whole body had become icy cold and he was trembling, but as he recovered, he quickly drew a rough sketch of what he had seen. Later he compared his drawing with pictures of Tudor ladies and found that the ghost's clothing was much the same in style. The dress was ground length with a bell-shaped skirt, tight at the waist, with a square neck and heavy, voluminous sleeves. He noticed further: 'The lady also wore a flowing veil attached to a circular head-dress fitted close to her head.'

Rycote's Grey Lady has been seen by several other people and on two occasions dogs have been seen to react, growling and showing signs of alarm at something apparently only they are aware of. So who was the mysterious Grey Lady? Sadly, no one seems to know.

16

❖❖❖❖❖❖❖❖❖❖❖❖❖

Haunted Pubs Galore

The Bear Inn at Woodstock dates back to the 12th century but many parts of the building have been added subsequently. Its haunted room is No. 16 where mysterious happenings have been experienced by visitors. Some have described being disturbed by the sound of footsteps on the old creaking floorboards and one occupant woke to find her dressing table light switched on, and some guests have found drawers opened and their possessions disturbed by an unseen phantom hand.

In the book *Ghosts of the Chilterns and Thames Valley* by Anne Mitchell (1972), there are said to be two ghosts, one connected with the 16th century murder of a woman in the cellar, and the other relating to a servant who, desperate to get rid of her illegitimate baby in the 17th century, stuffed the poor infant up one of the bedroom chimneys. There is, however, another version which may explain the sound of a baby crying when there is no child staying in the hotel.

It is said that centuries ago a rich and aristocratic lady and her maid arrived at the Bear on their way to Scotland. The lady was heavily pregnant and intended to give birth when she arrived at her destination, where she had planned to have her illegitimate child fostered in order to avoid scandal and the inevitable shame to her important family. But babies generally arrive in their own good time and this one was born prematurely at the inn, but with no skilled medical help on hand the poor child did not survive. This presented the lady and her servant with a terrible dilemma, and they concealed the body in a recess in Room 16. Since then guests have mentioned hearing the sound of a child's cries, and the ghostly apparition of a young woman has been seen around the hotel.

One night in 1976, several guests were still in the bar in the early hours at around 2.40 am when one young lady went upstairs to the ladies' room on the first floor. This is reached by a 16th century staircase, and within seconds she was heard to scream, and she came running downstairs gasping that there was the ghost of a woman on the landing. It was an exceptionally hot summer night, but when the porter went up to investigate, although he saw nothing, he noticed that the air had become 'deathly cold', but soon afterwards the temperature reverted to the previous stifling heat.

Two years later the night porter was sitting in his ground floor office when at 2.40 am he heard a crash on the upper floor. He went up and found a large plastic dustbin lid rocking gently on its handle about thirty feet away from the bin to which it belonged. A second bin beside it was untouched, and there was no one about.

Around 3 am seems to be the witching hour at the Bear, as on another occasion at this time the night porter was on his rounds checking the fire doors, but he found that each time he opened and closed a fire door, it would not stay closed. The restaurant manager noticed the porter's difficulty and was able to tell him that a ghostly lady was following him opening the fire doors as fast as he closed them!

One night the hotel manager's wife woke because someone was tugging at her duvet, and when she saw that a woman in black was responsible she screamed, which woke her husband. But he was unable to see the intruder before she disappeared. Many hopeful ghost-hunters who specially ask to stay in Room 16 are disappointed when no ghost pays them a visit, but everyone notices the chilly atmosphere, much colder than anywhere else in the hotel.

The George Inn at Wallingford is famous for its Teardrop Room, said to be haunted by the ghost of a landlord's daughter. One evening her lover arrived at the inn to see his sweetheart and is believed to have become involved in a brawl. It is known that in 1626, before the Civil War, Wallingford was full of soldiers, and because of their unruly behaviour a gallows was erected in the market place to enforce martial law. It is not known just what happened at the George, but the girl's sweetheart was murdered and the shock of the tragedy, which she witnessed, was too much for the poor girl, whose mind was so affected that she had to be confined to her room. While there she cried endlessly and, demented with grief, she mixed her tears with the soot from the fireplace and drew a design of pear shaped tears all over the wall.

The pub is believed to be haunted, and one woman guest woke in the night to see the figure of a weeping girl beside her bed. At first she thought it was a maid, and wondered why she was there, but then she felt a sensation of overwhelming sadness as the figure slowly turned away and disappeared through the wall. At the time the guest had not heard the story of the landlord's sorrowing daughter.

Many pubs with a ghost give them a name, and at the **White Hart in Minster Lovell** another sad figure is to be found – Rosalind, who sits veiled, crying bitterly, with her hands over her face. Tradition says that she was jilted by her sweetheart, and took her own life, and her ghost is seen close to an old spiral staircase which used to lead to the loft where it is believed she committed suicide.

The **George Hotel in Dorchester on Thames**, close to the Abbey Church, is sited on the foundations of what was probably the alehouse for the monks of the abbey. The inn's ghost here, too, is described as a tragic and sad-looking girl whose white figure has been seen as recently as 1971 in what is known as the Vicar's Room. Who she is and why she is so unhappy is unknown, but she is said to gaze miserably at the four poster bed before turning away and vanishing. It has been suggested that she or someone she loved may have died in that room.

The thatched and picturesque **Barley Mow at Clifton Hampden** also has a mysterious young woman ghost who was seen at Christmas 1970 in the pub car park. When two customers got into their car they noticed a pale face staring at them through the car window. There was something about the sudden appearance of the face and its transparency that suggested that this was no ordinary passer-by, and a few years later one of the car's occupants heard the story of Sarah Fletcher (see Chapter 17). She was told that Sarah's ghost was reputed to haunt the vicinity of Clifton Hampden, her former home, and felt sure that this was who she and her friend had seen.

The proximity of these two inns and the similarity of their ghost suggests that it is not impossible that they are both on the visiting list of the spirit of Sarah Fletcher, who has proved to be very active since her tragic death in 1799.

Lying between Banbury and Oxford, the **Holt Hotel near Steeple Aston**, a former coaching inn, is not only visited by the 17th century highwayman Claud Duval (see Chapter 21) but also has another ghost, a woman in black carrying a baby; she haunts a long corridor there, which is always icy cold. She is believed to be someone whose lover deserted her when she became pregnant, and deeply distressed by her disgrace she neglected the child, who died. She was charged and convicted of the baby's murder. Apparently quite recently a female guest came into the hotel very upset and said she had been drawing up outside when a woman in black had rushed across the road almost under her wheels. But, when she slammed on the brakes and got out of the car, there was no one there!

The **Catherine Wheel at Sandford on Thames** is haunted by a ghost believed to be a former landlord. He is sometimes seen leaning casually against the bar counter with his legs crossed and he wears black trousers, a black waistcoat and a white shirt.

Locals call him the Sandyman because he resembles the character which used to advertise Sandeman's port, a dramatic figure wearing a Spanish type of hat and black clothes.

The old **Angel Inn in Market Square, Witney** once had a piece of furniture with a hazardous reputation – a high wooden stool that had been the subject of a curse, mentioned in Joe Robinson's book *Oxfordshire Ghosts*.

The hero of the story was one Albert, a married man who nevertheless had a local reputation as a Casanova. Albert was never one to take no for an answer in his pursuit of the ladies of Witney, but on the day that his roving eye lighted on the wife of a local dignitary, Albert's fate was sealed. It was particularly unfortunate that the lady's husband was also a lay preacher whose homilies on the hell and damnation awaiting all transgressors put the fear of Judgement Day into many a Witney heart.

Albert and his lady love were engaged in romantic dalliance one day when they were appalled to hear footsteps on the stairs leading to the bedroom. The lady's husband had returned inconveniently early and Albert escaped through the bedroom window with practised speed. As it happened, there was a load of manure below which broke his fall, and Albert made for the Angel Inn, with nothing more than a damaged ankle and the all too obvious evidence of his less than happy landing!

But nemesis was on Albert's trail in the shape of one furious husband who, determined to wreak vengeance, burst into the Angel bar where Albert was sitting on the stool. A hefty fist rapidly sent the guilty lover flying backwards, to connect his head violently with the corner of the bar. It was the end of Albert, who with his dying breath cursed the stool and anyone who sat on it in the future.

Just what the stool had to do with Albert's misfortune is hard to see, but curse it he did, and since that day in the early 19th century local history relates that at least four people who risked Albert's curse came to sticky ends. The stool was eventually taken out of harm's way in 1847, and its present whereabouts are unknown, but the cautionary tale of amorous Albert, cut down in his prime, remains.

17

The Ghost with Red Hair

There are sad stories behind many hauntings, and this is no exception. But it is also the story of a man who fell romantically in love with a beautiful ghost. In the Dorchester Abbey church is a plain slab with this inscription:

*Reader! If thou hast a heart famed for Tenderness
and Pity, Contemplate this Spot in which are deposited
the Remains of a Young Lady whose artless Beauty,
Innocence of Mind, and gentle Manners once obtained
her the Love and Esteem of all who knew her. But when
Nerves were too delicately spun to bear the rude Shakes
and Jostlings which we meet with in this transitory World,
Nature gave way; she sunk and died, a Martyr to Excessive
Sensibility.*

MRS SARAH FLETCHER
Wife of Captain Fletcher, departed this life
at the village of Clifton on the 7th of June
1799 in the 29th year of her age.
May her soul meet that peace in Heaven which this earth
denied her.

But Sarah Fletcher did not rest in peace. Her spirit haunted her former home, 'Courtiers' in the village of Clifton Hampden, for many years. Sarah was married to a naval officer, a man with a roving eye, who apparently had become

70

so involved with a rich heiress that he was on the point of a bigamous marriage when Sarah heard about it, and was just in time to stop proceedings. It is easy to imagine the dramatic confrontation and recriminations, which caused the infamous Captain Fletcher to make a hasty retreat in the direction of his ship, on which he set sail for the West Indies, leaving the two ladies to cope as best they could.

Sarah returned home in such a desperately unhappy state of mind that she took her own life by tying her handkerchief to a piece of cord and hanging herself from the curtain rail of her bed.

Maude Ffoulkes, who compiled *True Ghost Stories* with the Marchioness Townshend, visited the Abbey church one summer day in 1913. She saw Sarah Fletcher's epitaph there and learned from the local vicar Sarah's intriguing story. She visited Courtiers, now an institution, but her enquiries about a ghost drew a blank. However, as she glanced down a passageway she saw a woman wearing a black cloak looking back at her. She had auburn hair tied with a ribbon, and her white face and anguished eyes made Maude feel that she was actually seeing the ghost of Sarah Fletcher.

Not much later her desire to know more was satisfied when she met a clergyman, Edward Crake, who had once lived in Courtiers and who shared her deep interest in Sarah Fletcher. Edward told Maude that his father was a schoolmaster, and when he was ten years old, his father rented Courtiers at an amazingly low rent, needing somewhere larger for his school and family. They soon discovered that previous tenants had never stayed there long, the property having an eerie reputation, but Mr Crake made it clear that he wanted no silly gossip about ghosts, which could be to the detriment of the school. For this reason Edward knew nothing about Sarah Fletcher until the night he actually saw her ghost, and fell in love with her.

It was a moonlight night. Edward was 17 and was lying in bed awake when he heard approaching footsteps. His bedroom door opened and he felt that someone unseen had entered, hesitated and gone out again. He heard the church clock strike three, and then as nothing else transpired he fell asleep.

The next night everything happened in just the same way, and he decided that the following night he would be ready to find out who or what the unseen intruder might be. Sure enough, just as before he heard the footsteps, and this time he felt sure it was the sound of someone in high heeled shoes. Once again the footsteps entered his room, approached his bed and then retreated. Edward jumped out of bed and ran out into the corridor, which was brightly lit by moonlight, and there for the first time he saw Sarah, standing by a window.

'She seemed tremendously alive,' he said. 'There was nothing "dead" about her. Her eyes were full of tears. She had come from the edge of the world, and from soundless space, to seek my love and pity.'

Maude asked what she looked like, anxious to confirm that when she visited Courtiers she, too, had seen the ghost of Sarah Fletcher. 'She wore a black silk cloak, fashionable at that period for protecting ladies' dresses from the dust of the roads,' remembered Edward. 'She was hatless, and her hair was twined about with a purple-red ribbon … I wanted to help her, to befriend her – then all at once a patch of moonlight alone marked the place where she had stood.'

Enquiries showed that other people in the house were aware of the ghostly footsteps, and an assistant master told Edward that once, when he was going upstairs, the footsteps approached him and he felt a cold wind pass by. On another occasion he heard the footsteps nearing his bed and saw a cloudlike mass which really frightened him.

Edward satisfied his curiosity about the lovely phantom by talking to a very old gentleman in the village who still remembered her 'artless beauty', and he also found a report of the inquest on 15th June 1799, which had reached a verdict of 'Lunacy', which made it possible for her to be buried in consecrated ground in the church. Edward and his friend, the assistant master, arranged to sit up all night on the anniversary of her death and keep a vigil.

At the usual time of quarter to three they heard footsteps descending the stairs, and, when his friend's courage failed him, Edward went on alone, hoping no doubt that once again he might see the beautiful Sarah. And it happened ... As he told Maude, 'Between the dawn on the one hand and the moon on the other, I saw her again. This time she smiled at me, and her face had lost something of its tragic intensity. She turned the handle of the door, opened it and I ran towards her ... she was so real that I could not believe I was in the presence of someone dead in the body for many years. "Speak to me," I begged, "please, please speak to me." But the door closed in my face, and when I pushed it open the room was empty except for a few boys sleeping quietly, unconscious of the phantom which had passed by.'

There were more occasional sightings of Sarah, and at other times Edward, still obsessed with his romantic dreams of the beautiful auburn haired ghost, sensed her nearness. Then, after about a year, the footsteps ceased, and there was a quieter more peaceful atmosphere in the house.

Ten years later, when Edward's brother had become the headmaster of the school at Courtiers, and he himself was now a clergyman, he received a letter from his brother asking him to come, as ghostly activity at the house had begun again in a more troublesome form. Occupants had been frightened by a presence at their bedside, and there was a lot of knocking and other noises.

Edward once again was captivated by a sighting of Sarah, and felt that, although there now seemed to be a malevolent power in the haunting, she was not the cause. But he could not ignore the violent disturbances and attempted an exorcism, which seemed to have a calming effect. However, this was shortlived, and people in the house often found themselves listening to what seemed to be furniture being moved about noisily overhead. Things came to a head when there was an outbreak of fever in the village, including the school, and in desperation Edward's brother decided to leave Courtiers and move his school to another town. Afterwards there were many tenants and considerable alterations to Courtiers over the years, and it eventually became a private residence again.

Edward Crake, who died in 1915, gave a report on the haunting of his old home to the Society for Psychical Research, but not his secret dreams about Sarah Fletcher which he had confided to Maude Ffoulkes. Is the sound of those little high heeled shoes still heard in the house where beautiful Sarah knew so much unhappiness? Does anyone now see the enchanting ghost with ribbons in her auburn hair?

Curiously enough, there was more to Sarah Fletcher's unusual story. When I went down to Dorchester recently and visited the Abbey Monastery Guest House Museum close by Dorchester Abbey church, I found there a small booklet about Sarah. It includes the experience of a Bournemouth landscape gardener who, while recovering from a serious illness, woke in the early hours of the morning to find his bedroom bitterly cold, although there was a heater on. He had the impression that there was someone else present, but decided that he must have been dreaming.

The next night he again woke from a dream, with the same feeling that there was someone in the room, but when he switched in his bedside lamp the room was empty, except for his wife asleep in the other twin bed. All was normal for the next few nights, but then he woke again feeling that someone had called him or tried to shake him awake, and the room was once again unnaturally cold.

He felt that there was something unusual about what was happening, and recalled the time when he was a child and he and his mother had woken in the night to see his granny, who had died some years earlier. He had also sometimes seen her subsequently and felt he could communicate with her telepathically. He wondered if perhaps his grandmother was visiting him again and he tried to thought-communicate with what he felt was a spirit at his bedside. But nothing happened and eventually he fell asleep once more. However, this time he had a dream about a young woman with 'startling brown eyes and very long tresses of beautiful hair, a radiant smile and a very outstanding figure'. And on waking he recalled the name Sarah and Dorchester Abbey church.

Determined to discover more about his strange experience, he drove to Dorchester in Dorset but could not discover any Dorchester Abbey church. Sometime later his wife found the book *True Ghost Stories* in the library, and there he read Maude Ffoulkes' account of Sarah Fletcher's story and found that the church where she was buried was in Dorchester, Oxfordshire.

The next time he woke feeling that there was a spirit in the room, he tried to reach out to it in his thoughts. 'If you are Sarah Fletcher, please give me a sign,' was the message he tried to communicate, and to his excitement the top cover of his bed was moved as if someone had pulled it away from him. He now felt sure that he was in contact with the ghost of Sarah Fletcher, but although he tried to get her to show herself the cold atmosphere warmed up and he knew she had gone.

Afterwards he was often conscious of her presence and he even had fleeting glimpses of her. He came to look upon Sarah as his guardian angel and believed she was looking after him. He tried without success to find her maiden name, as he wondered if they were related in some way, or whether they could have known each other in a previous life.

The story of Sarah Fletcher is an unusual and touching one. Edward Crake believed that she had returned to seek the love and pity that was denied her in life. And in the tender response to those whose hearts reached out to her, perhaps at last she found peace.

18

The Man Who Lost His Head

The headless ghost which traditionally haunted the churchyard at Farringdon is surrounded by a mystery. There are several versions of his history and, although the figure with his head tucked underneath his arm has not been seen within living memory, his origin and the strange story of his unfortunate fate remain an intriguing part of Farringdon's local history.

Farringdon House was the home of Sir Robert Pye Snr during the Civil War. He was a strong Royalist, but his son, also Sir Robert, was a leading Parliamentarian and was ordered by Fairfax to beseige his own father's house, which then surrendered in ruins in 1646. The church spire was also blown off, and some of the cannon balls fired against it are still on view in the church.

Sir Robert Jnr married the celebrated Roundhead John Hampden's daughter, Anne, and they had three sons, Hampden, Edmund and Richard, and several daughters. Richard died young, but Edmund became the apple of his parents' eye. Hampden, however, was something of a disappointment to his parents, and when his frequent carousing in local taverns led to his far too close relationship with a pretty young barmaid they were appalled. Even worse, when they pointed out the unsuitability of his consorting with someone so far beneath a gentleman of his social standing, he laughed in their faces, and divulged the amazing news that he and his paramour had just got married!

Before he could leave the house, Hampden was overpowered and locked in his room while his horrified parents debated the situation. They decided there was nothing for it but to send him away to join the navy. He must be removed from the clutches of his low-born consort. So, in no time, poor Hampden Pye found himself on board a ship bound for Spain under the command of Admiral Sir George Rooke.

It is here that the story takes a darker turn. In some versions Lady Pye is seen as the typical wicked stepmother, a woman who had always hated her stepson Hampden, whom she saw as a barrier to her own son inheriting the family fortune. One well-known account of the story is 'The Legend of Hamilton Tighe' in the *Ingoldsby Legends* by Thomas Ingoldsby, alias Sir Richard Harris Barham. But research shows that Sir Robert and Lady Anne Pye actually died within two months of each other in 1701 and there was never any stepmother, wicked or otherwise.

And yet the main point of the story is how the lady referred to as Wicked Lady Pye arranged with the captain of Hampden's ship to have him murdered. Why would his own mother do this? Some old versions of the story suggest that she was so possessively fond of Hampden that she could not bear to think of him married to the beautiful young barmaid, and so sent him to sea, and to his death.

This is said to have happened during a naval battle when to fulfil his mother's wishes the dastardly captain instructed a member of the crew to push Hampden in front of a stray cannon, with the result that his head was blown off.

Back in Farringdon, his mother and young Edmund were on their way to church for his memorial service when the ghost of Hampden appeared before them, his bloodstained head in his hands, causing his guilty parent to scream hysterically at the sight of what she had done and admit her guilt.

But here we come up against another discrepancy. Hampden's ship was said to be under the command of Sir George Rooke when his murder happened off the coast of

Spain. Sir George Rooke's expedition during the Wars of the Spanish Succession was in August 1702, sometime after Hampden's mother and father had died in 1701. Was Hampden's murder carried out regardless, or was his captain unaware that his parents were dead? And when did the dramatic scene where Wicked Lady Pye was confronted by the ghost of her murdered son happen?

Whatever the truth of Hampden's tragic death, his troubled spirit haunted Farringdon churchyard for a hundred years until the local vicar performed a service of exorcism with bell, book and candle, and he was finally able to rest in peace.

19

◆◇◆◇◆◇◆◇◆◇◆◇◆◇◆◇◆◇◆◇◆

Where Have All the Old Ghosts Gone?

A s everyone knows, all stately homes should have a ghost, but I have found some of Oxfordshire's old manor houses somewhat disappointing in this respect.

At Stanton Harcourt the manor's ghost is Lady Alice Harcourt, who was horribly murdered many centuries ago in the tower while the rest of the family were at mass in the chapel below. Tradition has it that the murderer was the chaplain, and the poor girl was hacked to pieces and her remains thrown down from the window. But there is no more information as to what lay behind this gruesome crime.

The tower is now known as Pope's Tower, as it was there that Alexander Pope, the poet, translated Homer's *Iliad* into English. On a pane of glass in the tower, he scratched the words: 'In the year 1789 Alexander Pope finished here the fifth volume of Homer.' Apparently he was happy to work in the tower although he knew about Lady Alice's fate and subsequent haunting, which he mentioned in a letter.

Lady Alice's ghost was said to haunt Stanton Harcourt between the chapel and the Lady Pool, where her ghost was apparently successfully laid after an exorcism.

Another ghost also joined Lady Alice in the Lady Pool. She was a Mrs Hall who committed suicide in the late 18th century by poisoning herself, heartbroken when she discovered her husband's affair with the landlady of the Harcourt Arms pub. She haunted the pub and also nearby Manor Farm, and was likewise exorcised into the Lady Pool. Both ghosts are said to return to their haunting if the Lady Pool ever dries up.

Stonor Park is intriguingly described as 'an area of high strangeness' and both Jack Hallam's *The Ghost Tour* (published 1967) and *Haunted Britain* by Anthony Hippisley Coxe (published 1973) recount a variety of ghostly happenings.

The sound of a man's footsteps was apparently heard overhead when no one was there. The footsteps then continued down the stairs to a room below, followed by the sound of a cupboard door being opened. Visitors to the house sometimes heard a knock on their bedroom door at night, and some had the alarming experience of waking to feel as if someone touched their face, or even scratched their forehead. And sometimes voices were heard coming from empty rooms.

Outside the chapel is the site of an ancient prehistoric stone circle, where a strange animal smell has sometimes been noticed, its origin hard to identify. And in the garden dogs have been seen to react to something that only they can see, which makes them growl and back away nervously. But when I enquired if these manifestations are still happening I was told that Stonor has no ghosts today!

Mapledurham mansion is haunted by the ghost of a servant murdered by his master in a fit of temper, an event still re-enacted at times when the murderer is seen dragging the corpse across the floor.

From medieval times there was a castle surrounded by a moat in Holton Park, five miles from Oxford. It was once occupied by Oliver Cromwell and his signature appears in the church register, when he was a witness at the marriage of his daughter Bridget to the Parliamentary commander, Henry Ireton. The castle and estate were bought in the 18th century by Elisha Biscoe, but when he discovered that the building was haunted he destroyed it and built the present house on a different site in the ground. In spite of this, apparently the ghosts moved into the new house and have been quite active.

In *The Oxfordshire Village Book* by the local Women's Institute it's said that according to local stories the ghost of a lady walks through the park and down to the village hall. She was a nanny who worked at the old manor house and one day when she was coming down the stairs carrying a baby she tripped or fell and unfortunately dropped the child, who was either killed in the fall or accidentally crushed by the weight of the nurse's body. The ghost is said to appear either in the early morning or late at night and has been frequently seen.

The ghost of a small black dog has also been seen – was it the dog which caused the nurse to trip on the stairs, perhaps?

At the house another ghost is described as a young boy in a dark blue velvet suit with a wide lace collar, believed to have been the heir to the manor. He was looked after by an uncle, his guardian, and according to legend his governess, with her eye on both the guardian and the estate, murdered the boy. Presumably the guardian was in league with her, and they buried the body in the garden south of the moat, where, years later, the new house was built. When the Biscoe family lived in the house, someone staying with them was standing at the foot of the stairs one evening when he saw a boy running towards him, but as he tried to intercept him the boy vanished.

There is a similar account in the book *Tyndale-Biscoe of Kashmir: An Autobiography* by Cecil Tyndale-Biscoe, in which the author mentions that when he was a boy he was standing at the foot of the stairs and, looking up, he saw a boy of about his own age hurtling rapidly down. He reached out to restrain him but the boy veered sharply round the bottom of the staircase to avoid him, and went off into the hall. Mr Tyndale-Biscoe noticed that the boy's feet didn't seem to touch the ground, and when he reached the hall, first his head and then the rest of his body 'went up suddenly in smoke, as if he had exploded'.

Park House eventually became Holton Park Girls' Grammar School, now Wheatley Park School. Does the boy in blue velvet or the little black dog still make an appearance among the pupils? It would be nice to know.

20

The Return of Miss Skene

On 2nd July 2002 a blue plaque was unveiled at 34 St Michael's Street, Oxford to commemorate Felicia Mary Frances Skene (1821–1899). Today many a passer-by may wonder just who she was, but in her day she was a familiar character in the city, a prison reformer, an author and philanthropist, and the first woman in England to be appointed an official prison visitor.

For the last twenty years of her life she visited Oxford Prison twice a week, and many women prisoners must have had reason to be grateful to her, as it was her habit to be at the gates to meet them on their release and take them to have breakfast, and later do her best to find them suitable work. She was a friend of Florence Nightingale, and when a cholera epidemic broke out in Oxford in 1854 she organised a band of nurses to help. She was described as a woman 'of strongly marked individuality and strongly marked features ... not easy to mistake' and it was a familiar sight in Oxford to see her striking figure striding briskly along, usually with a basket on her arm.

No doubt to Ernest Henham such a sight had been familiar since the days when as a schoolboy at St Edward's School he had often seen her there, as she was a friend of the warden, the Reverend Algernon Simeon, and often helped with the running of the school. So one winter afternoon in 1899 when he cycled from his home near Wallingford into Oxford and saw Miss Skene crossing the road ahead with her customary purposeful stride and usual complete disregard for traffic, he thought how well she looked and how remarkably vigorous she was for her age. He had intended to pay his old school a kind of nostalgic visit, so it was quite a coincidence to see someone from those days. He thought how much he would enjoy speaking to her again and decided to catch up with her.

But it was not to be. By the time he reached the pavement where she had been heading he was disappointed to find that she had disappeared among the other pedestrians. He was not to know that he would never see Miss Skene again, and that seeing her at all that afternoon was rather odd.

A biography of Miss Skene by E.C. Rickard was published in 1902 and, when he read it a year afterwards, it reminded Ernest Henham of the last time he had seen her. He remembered that afternoon quite clearly and felt sure it had been in the middle of November and yet, according to her biography, Miss Skene died on Friday 6th October 1899. Had he been mistaken in the date when he saw her in Oxford? Or had he perhaps seen some other elderly lady who resembled his old acquaintance?

But Ernest had no real doubt in his mind that it was Miss Skene he had seen; she was quite unmistakable and he had known her for years. And as for the date, his bicycle was a new purchase and he had the receipt dated 3rd October 1899. He was still learning to ride it when Miss Skene died on 6th October, and was certainly not experienced enough for a ride into Oxford. But how could he corroborate what had happened?

When he returned home that day he had casually mentioned seeing Miss Skene to his elderly aunt, but thought that at her age she would not now remember what he had told her back in 1899. But as it happened she had made a note in her diary of Ernest's 'little expedition' on his new bike, so was able to confirm that he had indeed cycled into Oxford on 15th November 1899.

So did Ernest Henham see the spirit of Miss Skene in Oxford more than a month after her death?

As ghost stories go, this lacks any particularly exciting ingredients, and yet by its very ordinariness it is all the more convincing that something supernatural happened that November afternoon. Did Ernest Henham experience a time warp in which he saw the familiar figure of Miss Skene striding through Oxford as she had so often done before? It was interesting to note that the woman he saw impressed him by how active she seemed for a woman in her late seventies, whereas towards the end of her life Miss Skene had become noticeably slower and more infirm. It is also interesting that Miss Skene was a member of the Society for Psychical Research and believed in supernatural apparitions. As she once said: 'How can we doubt them? With Dr Johnson I would say that if all reason is against it, the weight of evidence cannot be set aside. I hold that the world of spirits is closer to us than we are aware of, and if the veil were withdrawn from our eyes, we should see ourselves surrounded by a crowd of "ministering angels". To my mind there cannot be any doubt about the matter.'

21

❖◆❖◆❖◆❖◆❖◆❖◆❖◆❖◆❖◆❖◆❖◆❖

Stand and deliver

Held up by a Ghost!

The typical highwayman of the 17th and 18th century is usually seen as a romantic figure, daring and devil-may-care in his exploits, and always gallant to the ladies. In fact, the most famous one of all, Dick Turpin, was an unscrupulous thug, but after the Civil War the legend of the gentleman highwayman may have been due to the fact that many Royalists found themselves financially ruined and so had to take drastic measures to recoup their losses.

Oxfordshire had its fair share of gentlemen of the road, the most typical example of the charming rogue being Claud Duval, still fondly remembered at the Holt Hotel near Steeple Aston. The ubiquitous Turpin was said to frequent the George Hotel, in Oxford's High Street and also another George Hotel in Wallingford, but the old inns throughout the country that claim to have been Turpin hideaways are legion.

Three brothers, Tom, Dick and Harry Dunsdon or Dunstan, were also famous highwaymen in 18th century Oxfordshire, notorious for their skill at evading capture, for once they were able to reach Wychwood Forest their pursuers had no chance of finding them, as they knew every one of the area's useful boltholes.

On one occasion they intended to take cover at Langley Hall after an unsuccessful attempt to rob a stagecoach, but one of their gang had given them away to the authorities who were lying in wait for them at the hall and their life of crime almost ended there and then. However, poor Dick came to grief on this occasion when his hand became inextricably trapped somehow and his brother Harry had to cut off his arm to enable the brothers to escape. Some accounts say that Dick bled to death, but whatever the outcome his days on the road were over.

His two brothers continued their career for a time but it ended like that of many highwaymen, when they were caught and hanged in 1784. Some versions of the story say that they were hanged at Gloucester, and their bodies were later gibbeted from an oak tree on the edge of the forest they knew so well. Other reports suggest that they were actually hanged in Wychwood on 'Hangman's Tree', where their initials were carved, and that their skeleton remains suspended from a gibbet became a popular attraction for sightseers.

Around the old A40 road, now the B4047, between Minster Lovell and Burford, the ghost of a highwayman has been seen, known locally as 'Blackstockings' because this is what he wears! I found this unusual as most pictures of highwaymen show them in long leather riding boots. However, when I heard that Asthall Manor was once the home of a gentleman called Mr Freeman, and that he was reputed to have been a notorious masked highwayman who sometimes even robbed his own guests as they were either coming to the manor or on their way home, it seemed not unlikely that Mr Freeman and Blackstockings were one and the same. One can imagine that in his hurry to intercept his wealthy guests, he would ride out cloaked and masked, but with no time to change the breeches, stockings and buckled shoes he had been wearing in his more conventional role.

Not so long ago, a young lady on her way home to Fulbrook one night had just passed Worsham Bottom and was driving up the hill on the B4047, when she was startled to see right in front of her a rider on a black horse. The masked figure wore a tricorn hat and cloak, and flourished a flintlock pistol in his hand, and unlikely as it was, she realised that she was looking at a typical highwayman of centuries ago. She particularly noticed that he was wearing black stockings and shoes, not riding boots, and horse and rider both appeared entirely black in the moonlight.

Instinctively she drew up, and wound down the window for a better look, and at this the rider put away his pistol, wheeled his horse round the car and rode off soundlessly towards Worsham Bottom.

The whole experience seemed quite extraordinary, but on making enquiries afterwards she heard that there had been sightings of this phantom figure in the area for many years, and he was known locally as 'Blackstockings', as everyone who had encountered him had particularly noticed this rather unusual feature of his costume.

The Ladies' Joy

It was a bright, crisp day in the brilliant autumn of 2002 as we drove through the long tree-lined Cotswold lanes, russet, yellow and scarlet leaves on every side, the stone walls of the cottages golden as new baked loaves. Near Steeple Aston on the Oxford road I saw an inn sign showing a highwayman outside the Holt Hotel and knew I had come to the right place. There he was, not Dick Turpin claimed by so many inns as part of their history, but a rather different gentleman of the road, debonair, handsome Claud Duval, reputed to haunt the 15th century hotel ever since his encounter with Jack Ketch, the hangman, more than 300 years ago.

The Oxford road was a notorious rendezvous of highwaymen, including Duval, and it was said that he enjoyed spending his ill-gotten gains at the Holt Hotel, which, in the mid 17th century, was a busy coaching inn. There have been some changes in the building since those days. The bar where we had lunch is the old part and has a huge, almost lifesize painting of a highwayman, rear view, riding off on his nefarious business. Later the receptionist told me that this is where they are often aware of Duval's presence. Despite the cosy warmth there, was I fanciful to notice a sudden layer of cold air? And it was curious that the miniature bottle of tonic water beside my glass suddenly fell over for no apparent reason.

Claud Duval was not the aristocrat he liked to appear. He was born in 1643, the son of a Normandy miller, and it was as a servant to some of Charles II's supporters in Rouen, whom he accompanied back to England at the Restoration, and later as a footman to the Duke of Richmond, that he acquired the polished manners which charmed many an aristocratic lady. He soon took up the life of a highwayman and there were many tales told of his exploits.

Once, hearing that a certain wealthy man was travelling with £400 in cash, Duval lost no time in holding up the coach. The man's wife was there, and to demonstrate her cool indifference she produced a flageolet and played a light-hearted tune. This pleased Duval, who accompanied her on his own instrument, and then invited her to dance with him, which she did. Getting back to business, the highwayman cheekily suggested that the gentleman might like to pay for the music, and when he was given £100, he was so delighted by this that he let the couple keep the remaining £300 and sent them on their way. Macaulay described the unusual hold-up in his *History of England,* which inspired a painting by William Powell Frith in the Manchester City Art Gallery.

Duval's robbery of Charles II's Master of Buckhounds of 50 guineas in Windsor Forest was an unfortunate move, and he had to depart rapidly for France with a price on his head. But, plausible as ever, he tricked the King of France's Jesuit confessor into believing that he was an alchemist who could turn base metal into gold and managed to relieve him of a large haul of gold and jewels. Back in England he continued his career as a highwayman, card sharp and gambler, his good looks making him irresistible as always to the ladies. But his charmed life came to an end one day at the Hole-in-the-Wall Tavern in Chandos Street, near the Strand, when he was captured, too drunk to put up a fight.

He was tried on several charges on 17th January 1670, found guilty and sentenced to death, but despite pleas for his life, many from aristocratic ladies, the King had not forgotten the time that Duval robbed his Master of Buckhounds and would not consider the possibility of a pardon. And so on Friday, 21st January 1670, before a vast crowd, Claud Duval met hangman Jack Ketch at Tyburn. The end of many a villain in those days included a final farewell declamation but Ketch gave Duval no time for this, and a speech he had prepared in honour of his many women friends was found in his pocket after his death.

However, Duval was not denied his lying-in-state at the Tangier Tavern in St Giles, where, surrounded by candles, his body was guarded by men in black cloaks, and such huge crowds came to see him that a judge had to make an order to have them dispersed. He was buried under the centre aisle at St Paul's church, Covent Garden, his marble slab bearing this epitaph:

Here lies Du Vall, Reader, if male thou art,
Look to thy purse, if female, to thy heart,
Much havoc has he made of both, for all
Men he made stand, and women he made fall,
The second Conqueror of the Norman race,
Knights to his arms did yield, and ladies to his face,
Old Tyburn's Glory, England's illustrious thief,
Du Vall, the Ladies' joy, Du Vall, the Ladies' grief.

There were many colourful accounts of his life written afterwards, in which the charming rogue became the hero of many amazing exploits and his reputation as a great lover lost nothing in the telling. Talking to members of the staff at the hotel I was told that they were very aware of Claud 'all the time' and often noticed cold spots and shadows. But I had hardly hoped for a recent sighting!

Yet apparently a couple of weeks before my visit a Japanese lady guest had been standing alone in reception when a tall man in highwayman's garb passed through. When the receptionist returned the lady commented, 'What a good idea of the management to dress a member of the staff up as Claud Duval!' One can imagine her reaction when told that it was no member of staff that she'd seen. It was the real thing!

22

Never say 'baaaa'!

William Edden, nicknamed 'Noble', came to a sad end on his way home from Thame market one evening in 1828 because of his unfortunate sense of humour. Edden was a market gardener, who was working on his land one day, when he noticed two local bad lots, Sewell and Tylor, stealing a sheep from a neighbouring farmer's flock. At that time the penalty for sheep stealing was either transportation or death, and so Edden decided to keep quiet when police enquiries were made later. But he had no intention of letting the two thieves get away with their crime scot free.

So whenever he encountered Sewell and Tylor afterwards he couldn't resist baa-ing like a sheep. Needless to say the two thieves didn't see the joke at all, and although it amused Noble Edden to see their red faces and furious reactions he was soon to have reason to regret it, as they had quickly realised that they were totally dependent on his silence. And to men like Sewell and Tylor, there was only one certain way to be quite sure of that!

Did Edden perhaps have a presentiment that his joke had misfired? Setting out to return home from Thame market on the fateful night, he told a friend travelling with him that he feared something bad was about to happen to him. Concerned, his companion offered to continue all the way home with him, but Edden laughed it off and set his passenger down at his own farm as usual.

But Edden's premonition came true. Sewell and Tylor were lying in wait for him, and as he reached Anxey Bushes he was set upon and murdered.

Meanwhile Mrs Edden was at home in her farmhouse kitchen, ironing while she waited for her husband's return, so it was with a great sense of shock that she suddenly saw a terrifying vision appear in front of her. There was her husband and, unknown to him, another man appeared behind him, a heavy stone hammer in his hand. Mrs Edden gasped in horror as the man, whom she recognised as Tylor, raised the hammer and struck her husband down.

As this alarming vision faded, poor Mrs Edden rushed from the house screaming that her husband had been murdered, and when her neighbours came running they all set out at once to look for him. Noble's body was soon discovered, but it was too late – just as his wife had seen in her vision, he had been savagely bludgeoned to death. But although Mrs Edden was convinced that her husband's murderer was Tylor, just as certainly as if she had been there, a vision was not considered to be evidence. The verdict at the inquest was 'Murder by person or persons unknown'.

But the widow was not going to let the matter rest there. In those days it was believed that a murdered body would bleed at the touch of its killer, and in an attempt to prove his guilt Mrs Edden challenged Tylor to come and touch her husband's body. Not surprisingly, he could not be persuaded to do it.

Some time afterwards Edden's son was driving home when two men waylaid him in the dark, threatening to treat him as they had treated his father, but he managed to beat them off and escape, convinced by their voices that his attackers had been Sewell and Tylor.

Before long Sewell was imprisoned for a minor offence, and while in jail he hinted that Tylor was implicated in Edden's murder. Tylor was arrested but discharged for absence of proof, and, with an amazing lack of discretion, he expressed his delight by adorning his hat and coat with coloured ribbons and dancing around outside the houses of people who had given evidence against him.

But Sewell was an incorrigible rogue, and shortly after his release from prison he was back again for stealing hens. This time he was given a lengthy sentence of fourteen years transportation, and in an attempt to reduce it he went into more convincing detail about Edden's murder. He admitted that he had been there and had actually witnessed Tylor kill Edden with a stone hammer. The result was that this time both he and the partner he had betrayed were charged and found guilty.

On 8th March 1830 a huge crowd of 5,000 people gathered outside Aylesbury Prison to see Sewell and Tylor pay the ultimate penalty for the murder of Noble Edden. To the last Tylor swore that he was innocent, but in the light of Mrs Edden's prophetic vision and his partner's evidence there were few to believe him.

It seems sad that the earthbound spirit of the victim should linger at the scene of the crime, but tradition has it that should you encounter Noble Edden's apparition at the crossroads on the Thame to Aylesbury road it is a sign of good luck. Just don't say 'Baaaa'!

Bibliography

Deveneux, Paul *Places of Power: Measuring the Secret Energy of Ancient Sites*. Cassell Illustrated 1999

Ffoulkes, Maude *True Ghost Stories*. Senate Press 2002

Hallam, Jack *Ghost Tour*. Wolfe Publishing 1967

Hippisley Coxe, Antony D, *Haunted Britain*. Pan Books, 1973

Hole, Christina, *Haunted England*. C Chivers, 1972

Mitchell, Anne, *Ghosts along the Thames*. Spurbooks, 1972

Mitchell, Anne, *Ghosts of the Chilterns and Thames Valley*

Morris, A Clifford, *The Ryecote Yew*

Robins, Don, *Circles of Silence*. Souvenir Press Ltd, 1985

Roberts, J Aelwyn, *Holy Ghostbuster: A Parson's Encounters with the Paranormal*. Tegai Publishing, 1996

Robinson, Joe, *Oxfordshire Ghosts*. Wharncliffe Books, 2000

Tyndale-Biscoe, Cyril, *Tyndale-Biscoe of Kashmir: An Autobiography.*

Waldman, M, *Elizabeth and Leicester.*

Wentworth Day, James, *A Ghost Hunter's Game Book*. Muller, 1970

Index